P9-AGH-997

MORGAN · JAMES
PUBLISHING FOR THE REST OF US...
www.morganjamespublishing.com

Published by Morgan James Publishing, LLC
PO Box 6504, Newport News, Virginia, 23606 USA

ISBN: 0-9746133-8-X

Printed in the United States of America

DAVID L. HANCOCK

Guerrilla Marketing
for
Mortgage Brokers

David L. Hancock

2004

DAVID L. HANCOCK

Dedicated to those who use it!

DAVID L. HANCOCK

Table of Contents

DAVID L. HANCOCK

IMPORTANT

S ince the information within is top secret, please do not share this book with anyone else. You will only be aiding your competition.

First, thank you for your interest in Guerrilla Marketing for Mortgage Brokers.

This book was inspired by my friend Jay Conrad Levinson. Jay is the author of the best-selling marketing series in history, "Guerrilla Marketing," plus 27 other business books. His Guerrilla concepts have influenced marketing so much that today his books appear in 37 languages and are required reading in many MBA programs worldwide.

Jay taught Guerrilla marketing for ten years at the extension division of the University of California in Berkeley. And he was a practitioner of it in the United States — as Senior Vice-President at J. Walter Thompson, and in Europe, as Creative Director and Board Member at Leo Burnett Advertising.

He has written a monthly column for Entrepreneur Magazine, articles for Inc. Magazine, and writes online columns published monthly on the Microsoft Website – in addition to occasional columns in the San Francisco Examiner. He also writes online columns regularly for Onvia.com, FreeAgent.com, MarketMakers.com, and InfoUsa.com in addition to occasional columns for Guru.com.

Jay is the Chairman of Guerrilla Marketing International, a marketing partner of Adobe and Apple. He has served on the Microsoft Small Business Council and the 3Com Small Business Advisory Board. His Guerrilla Marketing is series of books, audiotapes, videotapes, an award-winning CD-ROM, a newsletter, a consulting organization, an Internet website, and a way for you to spend less, get more, and achieve substantial profits.

If you are interested in generating profits for your business, this is the right place for you to be looking. In every chapter, I give you valuable information that can contribute mightily to the profitability of your enterprise. If you take marketing and profitability seriously, you'll consult this book every week, and your new Guerrilla insights will soon be apparent on your profit and loss statement.

Until now, no marketing association in existence could make a business bulletproof. But once again, Jay Conrad Levinson, the most respected marketer in the world, has broken new ground. The Guerrilla Marketing Association is quite literally a blueprint for business immortality.

You've got to have it!

Join right now before your competition does at www.davidlhancock.com/gma.

Let's get started!

David L. Hancock
Certified Guerrilla Marketing Coach
www.DavidLHancock.com

What is Guerrilla Marketing?

G uerrilla marketing is unconventional strategies, secrets, and tactics for earning conventional goals — big profits from your small business. (If you think of your business in any other way you are mistaken.)

During the coming weeks, this Guerrilla marketing book will explore the 16 Guerrilla marketing concepts that guarantee success, the 100 Guerrilla marketing weapons, the structure for a seven-sentence Guerrilla marketing strategy and the ten steps you must take to succeed at a Guerrilla marketing attack.

Along with these concepts, the book will provide a flowing river of information that can make your marketing investment pay off handsomely while preventing you from wasting one cent of your precious marketing budget.

What is marketing in the first place?

Marketing is absolutely every bit of contact any part of your business has with any segment of the public. Guerrillas view marketing as a circle that begins with your ideas for generating revenue and continues on with the goal of amassing a large number of repeat and referral customers.

The three key words in that paragraph are EVERY, REPEAT, and REFERRAL. If your marketing is not a circle, it's a straight line that leads directly into the bankruptcy courts.

How is Guerrilla marketing different from traditional marketing?

Guerrilla marketing means marketing that is unconventional, non-traditional, not by-the-book, and extremely flexible.

There are eighteen factors that make it different from old-fashioned marketing:

1. Instead of investing money in the marketing process, you invest time, energy, and imagination.

2. Instead of using guesswork in your marketing, you use the science of psychology, actual laws of human behavior.

3. Instead of concentrating on traffic, responses, or gross sales, profits are the only yardstick by which you measure your marketing.

4. Instead of being oriented to companies with limitless bank accounts, Guerrilla marketing is geared to small business.

5. Instead of ignoring customers once they've purchased, you have a fervent devotion to customer follow-up.

6. Instead of intimidating small business owners, Guerrilla marketing removes the mystique from the entire marketing process and clarifies it.

7. Instead of competing with other businesses, Guerrilla marketing preaches the gospel of cooperation, urging you to help others and let them help you.

8. Instead of trying to make sales, Guerrillas are dedicated to making relationships. Long-term relationships are paramount in Guerrilla's success.

9.   Instead of believing that single marketing weapons such as advertising or a website work, Guerrillas know that only marketing combinations work.

10.   Instead of encouraging you to advertise, Guerrilla marketing provides you with 100 different marketing weapons; advertising is only one of them.

11.   Instead of growing large and diversifying, Guerrillas grow profitably and then maintain their focus, not an easy thing to do.

12.   Instead of aiming messages at large groups, Guerrilla marketing is aimed at individuals and small groups.

13.   Instead of being unintentional by identifying only mass marketing, Guerrilla marketing is always intentional, embracing even such details as how your telephone is answered.

14.   Instead of growing only by adding new customers, Guerrillas grow geometrically by enlarging the size of each transaction, generating more repeat sales, leaning upon the enormous referral power of customers, and add new customers.

15.   Instead of thinking of what a business can take, Guerrilla marketing asks that you think of what a business can give – in the way of free information to help customers and prospects.

16.   Instead of ignoring technology in marketing, Guerrilla marketing encourages you to be techno-cozy and if you're techno-phobic, advises you to see a techno-shrink because techno-phobia is fatal these days.

17.   Instead of being me marketing and talking about a business, Guerrilla marketing is you marketing and talks about the prospect.

18.   Instead of attempting to make a sale with marketing, Guerrilla marketing attempts to gain consent with marketing, then uses that consent to market only to interested people.

These are very critical differences and are probably the reasons that the concept of Guerrilla marketing has filled a void in the world's economy, explaining why the Guerrilla books have been translated into 37 languages, sold over one million copies, are required reading in most MBA programs, are available in audiotape and videotape versions, as computer software, as a nationally-syndicated column, as a newsletter, and are the most popular and widely-read marketing books in the world. Now, they're even available online.

GUERRILLA EXERCISE:

Compare your marketing with the 18 ways Guerrilla Marketing is different to see how many differences you already embrace. Your goal is to run your business by all 18.

Put a checkmark next to each difference your company puts into action:

1. I invest time, energy and imagination rather than only money.

2. My marketing is based upon psychology more than guesswork.

3. I measure my marketing performance by profits more than any other yardstick.

4. I embrace the principles of small business marketing more than large business marketing.

5. I follow-up all sales with customer contact and never ignore customers after they have purchased.

6. I am not intimidated by the marketing process and feel in control of my marketing.

7. My radar is attuned to cooperation in a quest to partner with others in co-marketing programs.

8. I tally up new relationships my company has made at the end of each month.

9. I employ combinations of marketing weapons rather than relying on only one.

10. I utilize a wide assortment of marketing weapons in the attainment of my business goals.

11. I am able to focus upon the main thrust of my business rather than looking for ways to diversify.

12. I direct my marketing to individuals and small groups more than large groups of people.

13. All of my marketing is intentional; I know marketing is any contact between my company and anyone else.

14. I strive to grow my company geometrically rather than linearly.

15. I freely give things away that can help my customers and prospects attain their own goals.

16. I use technology to strengthen my marketing and I have no fear of using it.

17. My marketing messages are stated from my prospects' and customers' points of view rather than my own.

18. My marketing attempts to gain consent from people to continue receiving my marketing materials.

GUERRILLA ACTION STEPS:

A. Review where you put checkmarks on the checklist above and circle the numbers at which no checkmark appears. These are the areas that need altering in your method of marketing.

B. Decide upon the specific actions that you will take for each statement so as to polish and perfect the performance of your marketing by transforming it into pure Guerrilla Marketing. List these in the space provided beneath each statement for which you have circled the number.

C. Take the actions you have listed, one by one, until each of the statements merits a checkmark. Your goal is a checkmark by each statement.

DAVID L. HANCOCK

The Secrets of Guerrilla Marketing

I f you memorize these 16 words and run your business by the concepts they represent, you will exceed your most optimistic goals.

The most important things you need to know about marketing are in this chapter. In the few minutes it takes you to read this, you'll learn more basic truths about marketing than you'd pick up with a score of MBA degrees under one arm and all the marketing books ever written, including mine, under the other.

As marketing continues to change, the secrets of Guerrilla marketing continue to change. Originally, there were three secrets, then seven, then twelve. Now, I'm going to clue you in on the 16 secrets that guarantee you will exceed your most hopeful projections, however dreamy they may be.

MEMORIZE THESE 16 WORDS THEN LIVE BY THEM.

I'm giving you a memory crutch so that you'll never forget these words, each one representing a major Guerrilla marketing secret. All 16 words end in the letters "ENT." Run your business by the Guerrilla concepts they represent and your marketing dreams will come true.

1. COMMITMENT: You should know that a mediocre marketing program with commitment will always prove more profitable than a brilliant marketing

program without commitment. Commitment makes it happen.

2.   INVESTMENT: Marketing is not an expense, but an investment – the best investment available in America today – if you do it right. With the 16 secrets of Guerrilla marketing to guide you, you'll be doing it right.

3.   CONSISTENT: It takes a while for prospects to trust you and if you change your marketing, media, and identity, you're hard to trust. Restraint is a great ally of the Guerrilla. Repetition is another.

4.   CONFIDENT: In a nationwide test to determine why people buy, price came in fifth, selection fourth, service third, quality second, and, in first place – people said they patronize businesses in which they are confident.

5.   PATIENT: Unless the person running your marketing is patient, it will be difficult to practice commitment, view marketing as an investment, be consistent, and make prospects confident. Patience is a Guerrilla virtue.

6.   ASSORTMENT: Guerrillas know that individual marketing weapons rarely work on their own. But marketing combinations do work. A wide assortment of marketing tools is required to woo and win customers.

7.   CONVENIENT: People now know that time is not money, but is far more valuable than money. Respect this by being easy to do business with and running your company for the convenience of your customers, not yourself.

8.   SUBSEQUENT: The real profits come after you've made the sale, in the form of repeat and referral business. Non-Guerrillas think marketing ends when

they've made the sale. Guerrillas know that's when marketing begins.

9.   AMAZEMENT: There are elements of your business that you take for granted, but prospects would be amazed if they knew the details. Be sure all of your marketing always reflects that amazement. It's always there.

10. MEASUREMENT: You can actually double your profits by measuring the results of your marketing. Some weapons hit bulls-eyes. Others miss the target. Unless you measure, you won't know which is which.

11. INVOLVEMENT: This describes the relationship between you and your customers – and it is a relationship. You prove your involvement by following up; they prove theirs by patronizing and recommending you.

12. DEPENDENT: The Guerrilla's job is not to compete but to cooperate with other businesses. Market them in return for them marketing you. Set up tie-ins with others. Become dependent to market more and invest less.

13. ARMAMENT: Armament is defined as "the equipment necessary to wage and win battles." The armament of Guerrillas is technology: computers, current software, cell phones, pagers, fax machines, wireless communications.

14. CONSENT: In an era of non-stop interruption marketing, the key to success is to first gain consent to receive your marketing materials, and then market only to those who have given you that consent. Don't waste money on people who don't give it to you.

15. AUGMENT: To succeed online, augment your website with offline promotion, constant maintenance of

your site, participation in newsgroups and forums, email, chat room attendance, posting articles, hosting conferences and rapid follow-up.

16.   CONTENT: Marketing is information that can benefit the lives of those to whom it is aimed, the truth made fascinating. If your marketing lives up to that definition, it has to be rich in content.

These 16 concepts are probably the reason that many start-up Guerrillas now run highly successful companies. They are the cornerstone of Guerrilla marketing. Just 16 words, but each one nuclear-powered and capable of propelling you into the land of your dreams.

GUERRILLA EXERCISE:

Measure your own company by how many of these concepts dictate your marketing. Compare them, one by one, with the way you currently run your marketing program. The idea is to run it by all 16.

Put a checkmark next to each of the Guerrilla principles that you understand and embrace to run the marketing of your business:

Commitment	Amazement
Investment	Measurement
Consistent	Involvement
Confident	Dependent
Patient	Armament
Assortment	Consent
Convenient	Augment
Subsequent	Content

GUERRILLA ACTION STEPS:

A. Review where you put checkmarks on the checklist above and circle the words at which no checkmark appears. These are the areas that need altering in your method of marketing.

B. Decide upon the specific actions that you will take for each "ent" concept so you can capitalize upon each secret of Guerrilla Marketing. List these in the space provided beneath each of the 16 concepts.

C. Take the actions you have listed, one by one, until each of the concepts merits a checkmark. Your goal is a checkmark by each concept.

Guerrilla Marketing Weapons

Your marketing arsenal can be much more potent than it is right now, it and won't even require much of an investment.

Ask the average loan officer what marketing is and you'll be told that it's advertising. Guerrillas know that this is nonsense. Advertising is only one weapon of marketing. How many weapons are most loan officers aware of? Maybe five or ten. How many do they use? Possibly three. But Guerrillas are aware of a full 100 Guerrilla marketing weapons and make use of about 40 of them. More than half of the weapons are free! Here, because this book wants you to be as lethal as possible, are ALL 100 weapons.

I present them in no particular rank or order because there's a 100-way tie for first place. Still, you will come across a few weapons that deserve red neon asterisks inside your head. Your job now as a loan officer is to do what you can to use as many weapons as possible.

1. Marketing plan

2. Marketing calendar

3. Niche/Positioning

4. Name of company

5. Identity

6. Logo

7. Theme

8. Stationery

9. Business card

10. Inside signs

11. Outside signs

12. Hours of operation

13. Days of operation

14. Package and label

15. Flexibility

16. Word-of-mouth

17. Community involvement

18. Neatness

19. Referral program

20. Sharing with others

21. Guarantee or warranty

22. Telemarketing scripts

23. Gift certificates

24. Printed brochures

25. Electronic brochures

26. Location

27. Advertising

28. Sales training

29. Networking

30. Quality

31. Reprints and blow-ups

32. Flipcharts

33. Opportunities to upgrade

34. Contests/sweepstakes

35. Barter options

36. Club memberships

37. Partial payment plans

38. Phone demeanor

39. Toll-free number

40. Cause (environment)

41. Free consultations

42. Free seminars

43. Free demos or tours

44. Free samples

45. Giver vs. taker stance

46. Fusion marketing

47. Marketing on hold

48. Past success stories

49. Attire

50. Service

51. Follow-up

52. Yourself and your employees

53. Free gifts

54. Catalog

55. Yellow pages ad

56. Column in a publication

57. Article in a publication

58. Speaker at a club

59. Newsletter

60. All your audiences

61. Benefits of your offering

62. Computer

63. Selection

64. Contact time with customers

65. How you say hello and goodbye

66. Public relations

67. Publicity contacts

68. Online marketing

69. Classified ads

70. Newspaper ads

71. Magazine ads

72. Radio commercials

73. TV spots

74. Infomercials

75. Movie commercials

76. Direct mail letters

77. Direct mail postcards

78. Postcard for postcard deck

79. Outdoor billboards

80. Fax-on-demand (or email-on-demand)

81. Special events

82. Show displays and staff

83. Audio-visual aids

84. Posters

85. Prospect mailing lists

86. Research studies

87. Competitive advantages

88. Marketing insight

89. Speed

90. Testimonials

91. Reputation

92. Enthusiasm

93. Credibility

94. Spying on self and others

95. Easy to do business with

96. Brand name awareness

97. Designated Guerrilla

98. Customer mailing list

99. Competitiveness

100.   Satisfied customers

These 100 weapons should be considered for every Guerrilla's arsenal. Once you've selected them, put them into priority order, set a date for the launching of the weapon, and appoint a person to mastermind your use of the weapons you've selected. Whatever you do, launch your Guerrilla marketing attack IN SLOW MOTION, only launching weapons when you can utilize them properly at a pace that is comfortable emotionally and financially. After launching, KEEP TRACK because some weapons will hit bull's-eyes while others will miss the target. Unless you keep track, you won't know which is which. Guerrillas always know which is which.

GUERRILLA EXERCISE:

Review each weapon and place it into one of four categories: Using Properly Now, Using But Needs Improvement, Not Using But Should, Not Appropriate Now. Your job is to work at your marketing so as to make the first category as lengthy as possible and to eliminate the second and third categories completely.

Total the number of weapons in each category:

Weapons I use properly now...

Weapons that need improvement...

Weapons I don't use, but should...

Weapons not appropriate right now...

The total of all four categories is: 100

GUERRILLA ACTION STEPS:

A. List the weapons that need improvement.

B. Make the improvement in your use of each of those weapons.

C. List the weapons you don't use, but should.

D. Launch each weapon you deem appropriate for your business at this time.

You need not utilize all 100 weapons, but you do need to improve the weapons requiring improvement, and you should be using all the weapons you believe can help increase your profits.

The Newest & Most Potent Marketing Weapon: Memes

A Meme is The Lowest common denominator of an idea; A basic unit of communication. A Meme alters human behavior, motivates people. It is simplicity itself; understandable in seconds. A Meme is graphic using words or action.

One of the most powerful and ancient memes in history was the wheel. A wagon with spoke wheels carries not only freight from place to place – it also carries the unmistakable idea of a wagon with spoke wheels from mind to mind.

Many other non-marketing memes have made their way into our culture. The hula hoop, snowboarding, rollerblading, miniskirts, Beatle haircuts, bottled water — a long list of concepts such as these seem to roar through the community like a brush fire.

Even the word "God" is a meme because it reduces the enormous idea down to a single word, which represents the entire concept of belief in a supreme being. To understand memes even better, consider how memes compare with beliefs:

Beliefs are feelings of certainty about what something means.

Memes are sources of information, which created that feeling of certainty.

Beliefs are effects. Memes are causes.

Beliefs are attitudes that spring from ideas. Memes are simplified representations of ideas.

Beliefs are feelings or inclinations. Memes are basically icons with an implied subtext.

Beliefs are internal. Memes are external until they replicate. When they do, they become internalized and develop into beliefs.

Beliefs can last a lifetime and might take a while to enter a mind. Memes invade the mind in an instant and don't necessarily last a lifetime. In marketing, however, they ought to be created to last a lifetime.

Beliefs are expanded attitudes about life. Memes are compressed and transmissible packets of information.

Beliefs usually take a while to grasp entirely. Memes are the quickest and most effective ways to transmit and receive complex concepts from one mind to another.

Beliefs require conscious consideration. Memes are transmitted in a moment.

The best-known memes of the 20th century:

1. The Marlboro Man - Marlboro cigarettes

2. Ronald McDonald - McDonald's restaurants

3. The Green Giant - Green Giant vegetables

4. Betty Crocker - Betty Crocker food products

5. The Energizer Bunny - Energizer batteries

6. The Pillsbury Doughboy – Assorted Pillsbury foods

7. Aunt Jemima – Aunt Jemima pancake mixes & syrup

8. The Michelin Man – Michelin tires

9. Tony The Tiger – Kellogg's Frosted Flakes

10. Elsie The Cow – Borden dairy products

All but one of these campaigns was around long before Dawkins invented the word "meme." Each of the memes mentioned above represents an entire idea. Memes are always ideas, but ideas are not always memes.

But if the ideas are distilled, compressed, simplified and focused, then presented in a manner that can be communicated through a wide range of media – from the Internet to a billboard – they might become memes.

But not all great ideas or great marketing campaigns furnish us with a meme. To see this up close and personal, study the top ten slogans of the past century, again selected by Advertising Age. Some have memes. Some do not. Those with memes tell us about the product being marketing. Those without memes tell us nothing about the product or its benefits.

The top ten slogans of the 20th century

1. Diamonds are forever (DeBeers) – The three words are a meme.

2. Just do it (Nike) – No meme here, just three words.

3. The pause that refreshes (Coca-Cola) – Definitely a meme.

4. Tastes great, less filling (Miller Lite) – A meme without question.

5. We try harder (Avis) – A meme telling us about the company.

6. Good to the last drop (Maxwell House) – A meme about the product.

7. Breakfast of champions (Wheaties) – Another meme about the product.

8. Does she... or doesn't she? (Clairol) – A meme at work.

9. When it rains it pours (Morton Salt) – A meme with a visual.

10. Where's the beef? (Wendy's) – A short-lived meme – if a meme at all.

To show you that social conscience rarely entered into a person's purchasing behavior, notice how the top ten includes an air polluter (Avis), nutrition-less sugar water (Coca-Cola), one reviled carcinogen (Marlboro), two companies infamous for the use of virtual slave labor (DeBeers, Nike), one purveyor of savory cardiovascular time bombs (McDonald's), one booze peddler (Miller-Lite), one product that is laced with caffeine (Maxwell House), and one cosmetic product preying on vanity (Clairol).

Fortunately, cause-related marketing is coming to the fore.

To get your meme consciousness into even higher gear, consider the slogans selected for honorable mentions:

- Look Ma, no cavities! (Crest toothpaste) – Meme about product.

- Let your fingers do the walking (Yellow Pages) — Meme with visual.

- Loose lips sink ships (public service) – Meme with visual.

- M&Ms melt in your mouth, not in your hand (M&M candies) – Meme

- We bring good things to life (General Electric) – Not really a meme.

GUERRILLA EXERCISE:

Create a Meme using verbal and visual clues.

Guerrilla Marketing Strategy

Running a business without a marketing strategy is like driving into a new nation without a roadmap to guide you.

I am flabbergasted that so many loan officers operate without a marketing strategy. It's like entering battle under a commander who orders you: READY! FIRE! AIM! A Guerrilla marketing strategy prevents hit and miss marketing and enables you to hit the bull's-eye of your target with every single shot you take.

A Guerrilla marketing strategy has only seven sentences. It is brief because of two important reasons. Number one, a seven-sentence strategy forces you to focus, and number two, everyone in your organization can read and understand a simple seven-sentence marketing strategy, putting them smack dab on your wavelength. Proctor and Gamble may be the most sophisticated marketing company on the planet. All their brands are guided by brief, seven-sentence strategies.

They may have 50 more pages of documentation, but the focus is winnowed down to seven sentences. And only one of them has to be a long sentence.

For an example I won't use the mortgage business so you won't be tempted to skip this ultra important step so let's say you run a service that teaches people how to operate computers. Let's say the name of your company is Computer Tutor. And finally, let's say you have the mind and goals of a

Guerrilla. Here's how a Guerrilla marketing strategy would work for you.

1. The first sentence tells the purpose of your marketing.

The purpose of Computer Tutor marketing is to book 100% of the company's available time for computer education at the lowest possible cost per hour.

2. The second sentence tells how you'll achieve your purpose, concentrating upon your benefits and your competitive advantage or advantages.

This will be accomplished by establishing the credentials of the educators, the location of the operation, and the training equipment.

3. The third sentence tells your target audience — or audiences.

Our target market is local small business owners who can benefit from learning to operate a computer; our secondary market is large corporations.

4. The fourth sentence tells the marketing weapons you'll use.

Marketing weapons to be utilized will be a combination of personal letters, circulars, brochures, signs on bulletin boards, classified ads in local newspapers, yellow pages advertising, direct mail special offers, advertising specialties, free seminars, sampling, a referral program, telephone training, professional office decor and employee attire, a website offering a free newsletter, and publicity in the local newspapers, on radio talk shows, and on television.

5. The fifth sentence tells your niche in the market.

We will position ourselves as the prime source of one-on-one, guaranteed instruction in the operation of small computers.

6. The sixth sentence tells your identity.

Our identity will be a blend of professionalism, personal attention, and warm, human regard for our students and the role of computers in their lives and their businesses.

7. The seventh sentence tells your marketing budget as a percent of your projected gross sales. (The average U.S. business invested 4 percent.)

Ten percent of projected gross sales will be allocated to marketing.

This strategy should guide your efforts for the next one to fifty years. Use it to measure ALL marketing materials you plan to use. No matter how much you may love them, if they do not fulfill your strategy, toss them right into your wastebasket.

You should review your Guerrilla marketing annually and make slight tweaks in it, especially in the fourth sentence, but the idea is to get it right the first time, then commit to it – making sure all your employees and co-workers read it and know what you're up to. You'll be up to earning record-breaking profits, and the bright light of your Guerrilla marketing strategy will illuminate your path.

GUERRILLA EXERCISE:

Write a seven sentence Guerrilla marketing strategy for your business. Follow the format I've just described, then pin the written strategy up inside your head.

1. The purpose of my marketing is:

2. I will accomplish this purpose by stressing my:

3. My target audience or audiences is:

4. Marketing weapons I plan to employ are:

5. My niche in the marketplace is:

6. My business identity is:

7. I plan to devote ____% of gross sales to marketing.

GUERRILLA ACTION STEPS:

A. Show your completed marketing plan to everyone in your organization who is involved with marketing.

B. Show your completed marketing plan to each of your employees, even if they are not involved with your marketing.

C. Breathe life into your plan by doing exactly what you say you will do and measuring all your marketing materials, current and future, against the strategy. If they do not follow the strategy, change them or discard them.

DAVID L. HANCOCK

Guerrilla Marketing
Personality Traits

Guerrilla Marketers are both born Guerrillas and made Guerrillas. If they lack these traits, they work to develop them.

While Jay Conrad Levinson was working with the marketing honchos of Fortune 500 companies *(and the marketing chiefs of new up-and-coming companies that want like crazy to be members of the Fortune 500)* he noticed eight personality traits that these marketing geniuses possessed. And try as I may, I simply have not found an exception to this Guerrilla observation. People who run successful marketing departments have every one of these eight characteristics.

I hope that you already have all eight of these personality traits, or that you can at least develop the one or two that may be lacking. Otherwise, I urge you to turn the task of marketing over to somebody else because marketing is going to get you in trouble and the way you use marketing will get your company in trouble. Let's examine the eight right here and right now:

1. PATIENCE: I start with this trait because it's the most important by far. A study was conducted to see how many times you must penetrate a person's mind with your selling proposition before you convert that person from a state of total apathy to a state of purchase readiness. Amazingly, the researchers

came up with an answer. It was nine. Your message must penetrate a mind nine times before that person will buy what you are selling. And that's the good news. The bad news is that for every three times you put out the word, your prospects are paying attention only two times.

So you market by advertising, emailing, telemarketing, signs, direct mail, anything – and you put the word out three times and it penetrates your prospect's mind one time. What do you suppose happens? Nothing happens. Zilch. Okay, you put the word out six times, entering the mind of your prospect two times. What happens then?

Again, not one thing happens. All right, now you put the word out nine times and you have penetrated the mind of your prospect three times. What happens?

Your prospect knows he or she has heard of you before. That's what happens. No sale. No cigar. Not yet at least.

Sticking with the drill, you put out the word twelve times and your prospect's mind has been pierced four times. What happens then? What happens is that your prospect realizes he or she has seen your marketing before and people figure that if they keep seeing your marketing, you must be doing something right. But still, nobody is buying anything.

Now, you put out the word 15 times and penetrate your prospect's mind five times. At this point, the prospect probably reads every word of your ad or letter, probably even sends away for the brochure you've been offering all along. At this point, most small advertisers figure they've been doing everything wrong and so they abandon their marketing program. DON'T DO IT! NOT YET! This horrid state of affairs is called sellus interruptus. The sale is never consummated because the marketing chief didn't have the patience to hang in there.

After you've put the word out 18 times, and you've penetrated a mind six times, the person begins to think of when they'll make the purchase. Put out the word 21 times and you've penetrated a mind seven times. The person begins to think of where they'll get the money and how they'll pay. Put out the word 24 times and the prospects, with their minds penetrated eight times, write in their date book when they will buy from you. They check with whoever they must check with before making a purchase. Finally, you get the word out 27 times; penetrate your prospects' minds nine times they buy from you. Eventually, the profits come rolling in.

Think that process can take place if you have no patience?

NO WAY.

That's why patience remains the most important of the eight personality characteristics.

2. IMAGINATION: This doesn't necessarily refer to headlines or graphics or jingles or being clever as much as it does facing up to reality. If you're going to do a direct mailing, face up to the fact that everyone and their cousin does direct mailings. Why should your envelope get opened?

Because you've got the imagination to pop for first class postage and to put twelve stamps on your envelope – a 6-center, four 4-centers, a 3-center, and six 2-centers. Who could resist opening an envelope with eleven stamps? Not only will it be opened, but it will be opened first. Doesn't take a lot of money, does takes a powerful imagination.

3. SENSITIVITY: People who run first-rate marketing shows are sensitive to their market, their prospects, the economy, the community, and the competition. It's a key personality trait.

4. EGO STRENGTH: The first people who will tire of your marketing program will be your co-workers, followed closely by your employees, your family, and

your friends. They will counsel you to change because they are bored. Your prospects are not bored and have barely heard of you. Your customers will not be bored and will forever read your marketing materials to justify the fact that they still do business with you.

5. AGGRESSIVENESS: You need to be aggressive in your spending and your thinking. When you hear that the average U.S. business invested 4 percent of gross revenues in marketing in l999, you want to invest 6 percent, 10 percent. When you hear there are 100 marketing weapons, you want to use at least half of them.

6. CONSTANT LEARNING: A seagull flies in endless circles, seeking food. When it finds food, it eats its fill, then flies in circles again, looking for more food. Seagulls just have to look for food. Humans have one instinct that is just as strong. Know what it is? To learn. Successful Guerrillas know a lot, but keep learning more.

7. GENEROSITY: Guerrillas view marketing as an opportunity to help their prospects and customers succeed at their goals, whatever they may be. They think of things they can give away to help those people. They are generous with their time and their information.

8. TAKE ACTION: Many people read books, hear tapes, take courses and attend seminars. But most of them keep this information within them. Guerrillas learn the very same ways, but take action based upon what they have learned. They know that action is the power behind Guerrilla marketing.

Those are the eight and the only eight traits that great marketing directors seem to have in common. I sure hope all eight apply to you.

GUERRILLA EXERCISE:

Benjamin Franklin said that the three hardest things in the world are diamonds, steel and knowing yourself. Compare the eight Guerrilla personality traits with your own, and then be honest in knowing which ones you must develop even more.

Put a checkmark next to each of the Guerrilla marketing personality characteristics that you possess. The character traits that I currently have are:

Patience

Imagination

Sensitivity

Ego strength

Aggressiveness

Constant learning

Generosity

Take action

GUERRILLA ACTION STEPS:

A. Circle each personality trait that does not have a checkmark.

B. Begin developing those traits in yourself.

C. Put a checkmark next to each trait that you are able to develop. The goal is to have a checkmark next to each trait.

The Guerrilla Marketing Attack

Mounting a Guerrilla Marketing attack is a process that begins with the easy parts, and then asks more of you as the attack gains momentum.

Succeeding with a Guerrilla marketing attack is a very intense ten-step process. Take all ten steps and watch your profits rise and your competitors cringe.

It's not as hard as you may think to succeed at a Guerrilla marketing attack. And if you launch one properly, you'll find that succeeding at business is also not as hard as you may have thought. Don't even think of skipping any of the ten steps to success because all ten are necessary. We're not talking about playing with marketing. We're talking about succeeding with marketing.

The first step is to research everything you can. That means carefully investigating your market, your product or service, your competition, your industry and your options in media. It means looking into the benefits you offer, into the latest technology and into the makeup of your existing customers. What media reach your target audience? What media makes them respond and buy? Should you focus on advertising or direct marketing or a combination of the two? Do you need a website and if so, why?

1. There are answers to these questions and Guerrillas have the knack for coming up with the right answers. As a person who is already connected to the

Internet, you've got a head start in the research department. There is loads of information online that can propel you in the direction of success.

2. The second step is to write a benefits list. Have a meeting. Invite your key personnel and at least one customer – because customers are tuned in to benefits that you may not even consider to be benefits. Example, my wife patronizes a certain bookstore regularly, not because of their books, but because of the carrot cake they serve in their cafe. Once you have a list of your benefits, select your competitive advantage because that's where you'll hang your marketing hat. If you haven't got a competitive advantage, you'll have to create one because you'll need it. After all, anyone can come up with a benefits list. Figure out why people should patronize your business instead of a competitor.

3. Step number three is to select the weapons you'll use. In my fourth Guerrilla marketing online class, I listed an even 100 weapons from which you may make your selection. My recommendation is to use as many weapons as you can. More than fifty of the hundred weapons are free. After you've selected the weaponry, put the weapons into priority order. Next to each weapon, write the name of the person who is in charge of masterminding the use of the weapon plus the date it will be launched. Consider each date you write to be a promise you are making to yourself. Guerrillas do not kid themselves or lie to themselves, so be realistic.

4. The fourth step is to create a Guerrilla marketing strategy. The way to do this is elaborated upon in detail in Guerrilla Marketing Lesson Four. I'll let you find it later rather than taking your time right now.

5. Step five is to make a Guerrilla marketing calendar. This should be 52 rows long and five columns wide.

The first column is called "Month" – listing in which month of the twelve you did what you did in marketing. The second column is called "Thrust" – referring to the thrust of your marketing that week. What were you saying? Offering? The third column is called "Media" and it refers to which media you were using that month. The fourth column is called "Cost" and lets you project how much you'll be spending that month. The fifth column is called "Results" so you can give a letter grade to the month – you know, an A, B, C, D or F. After one year, you compare your calendar to your sales figures and eliminate all but the A's and B's. It takes about three years to get a calendar loaded with slam dunks. Once you have one you'll feel like the client who said of his, "It's a lot like going to heaven without the inconvenience of dying." I'll give you a copy of my Guerrilla marketing calendar if you just ask by sending me an email to gmcalendar@davidlhancock.com.

6. Step six is to locate fusion marketing partners, businesses with the same prospects and the same standards as you have. Offer to go in on co-marketing ventures with them. Trade links online. Trade lead lists each month. The motto of the millennium: fuse it or lose it.

7. This is the step when you launch your Guerrilla marketing attack. The idea of a Guerrilla marketing attack is to select a lot of weapons, then launch them in slow motion – at a pace that feels comfortable financially and emotionally. My average client takes 18 months to launch an attack. Don't rush.

8. The eighth step, and this is a toughie, is to maintain the attack. The first seven steps are extremely simple compared to this step. Maintaining the attack

means sticking with your plan and your weapons even though you don't get the instant gratification you want so much. Everyone wants success to come instantly, but it doesn't happen that way in real life. The Marlboro Man and Marlboro Country helped make Marlboro cigarettes the most successfully marketed brand in history. But after the first year of marketing, they didn't increase sales one bit for Marlboro. Maintaining the attack made it happen.

9. Step nine is to keep track. Some of your weapons will hit bulls-eyes. Others will miss the target completely. How will you know which is which? By keeping track. By asking customers where they heard of you. By finding out what made them contact you. Keeping track is not easy, but it is necessary. If you aren't ready to keep track, you aren't ready to launch your attack in the first place.

10. The tenth and final step is to improve in all areas: your message, the marketing weapons you're using, and your results. A Guerrilla Marketing attack is a never ending process. But it works every time.

That's it. Ten steps to succeeding with a Guerrilla marketing attack. If it sounds easy, reread this lesson. It works, but it's not easy.

GUERRILLA EXERCISE:

Take the first five steps right now. Begin to take the sixth. Then, you'll be prepared for victory when your attack is in full force. Putting your attack into writing with this exercise will give wings to your dreams.

Check each step of the Guerrilla marketing attack that you have taken or will take:

I have done the proper research.

I have written a benefits list.

I have selected the marketing weapons I will employ.

I have written my marketing strategy.

I have prepared my marketing calendar.

I have located fusion marketing partners.

I have launched my attack at a comfortable pace.

I am able to maintain my attack.

I am able to keep track of each weapon's effectiveness.

I have improved each facet of my Guerrilla marketing attack.

GUERRILLA ACTION STEPS:

A. Review where you put checkmarks on the checklist above and circle the statements at which no checkmark appears. These are the areas that you must focus upon to succeed with your attack. Be aware of them.

B. Decide upon the specific actions that you will take for each statement so as to mount an effective Guerrilla marketing attack. List these in the space provided beneath each statement for which you have circled the number.

C. Take the actions you have listed, one by one, until each of the statements merits a checkmark. Your goal is a checkmark by each statement. An incomplete attack is a recipe for failure.

D. Request a copy of my Guerrilla marketing calendar by sending me an email to gmcalendar@davidlhancock.com

Guerrilla Marketing: What Marketing is Not

Marketing is all contact from anyone in your company with anyone outside of your company. It's a process and not an event.

Guerrillas know that marketing is just a fancy word for selling and treating people well. It is more common sense and patience than anything else. But people think marketing is a bunch of things it isn't. Let's look at what marketing is not.

1. Marketing is not advertising. Don't think for a second that because you're advertising, you're marketing. No way. There are over 100 weapons of marketing. Advertising is one of them. But there are 99 others. If you are advertising, you are advertising. You are doing only 1% of what you can do.

2. Marketing is not direct mail. Some companies think they can get all the business they need with direct mail. Mail order firms may be right about this. But most businesses need a plethora of other marketing weapons in order for their direct mail to succeed. If you are doing direct mail only, you're no Guerrilla.

3. Marketing is not telemarketing. For business to business marketing, few weapons succeed as well as telemarketing – with scripts. Telemarketing response can be dramatically improved by augmenting it with

advertising, yes, advertising, and direct mail, yes, direct mail. Marketing is not telemarketing — alone.

4. Marketing is not brochures. Many companies rush to produce a brochure about the benefits they offer, and then pat themselves on the back for the quality in the brochure. Is that brochure marketing? It is a very important part when mixed with 10 or 15 other very important parts – but all by itself? Forget it.

5. Marketing is not the yellow pages. Most and I mean most companies in the U.S. run a yellow pages ad and figure that takes care of their marketing. In 5% of the cases, that's the truth. In the other 95%, it's disaster in the form of marketing ignorance. Sure, have a yellow pages ad as part of your arsenal. But only part.

6. Marketing is not show business. There's no business like show business, and that includes marketing. Think of marketing as sell business, as create-a-desire business, as motivation business. But don't think of yourself as being in the entertainment business because marketing is not supposed to entertain as much as it is to generate honest profits.

7. Marketing is not a stage for humor. If you use humor in your marketing, people will recall your funny joke, but not your compelling offer. If you use humor, it will be funny the first and maybe the second time. After that, it will be grating and will get in the way of what makes marketing work — repetition.

8. Marketing is not an invitation to be clever. If you fall into the cleverness trap it's because, unlike the Guerrilla, you don't realize that people remember the cleverest part of the marketing even though it's your offer they should remember. Cleverness is a

marketing vampire, sucking attention away from your offer.

9. Marketing is not complicated. It becomes complicated for people who fail to grasp the simplicity of marketing, but marketing is a user-friendly to Guerrillas. They begin with a seven-sentence Guerrilla marketing plan, create a marketing calendar, and select from 100 weapons. Not too complicated.

10. Marketing is not having a website. A website may turn out to be your single most valuable marketing weapon, but all by itself, it is not marketing. In fact, it must be marketed with the same energy you use to market your primary offering.

11. Marketing is not a miracle-worker. More money has been wasted due to marketers expecting miracles than to any other misconception of marketing.

Marketing is the best investment in America if you do it right and doing it right requires commitment, patience and planning. Expect miracles get ulcers.

Before I let you scour the Net for more nuclear-powered gems for your business, I feel honor-bound to let you know that marketing is an opportunity for you to earn profits with your business, a chance to cooperate with other businesses in your community or your industry, and a process of building lasting relationships.

Marketing is a topic that intimidates many business owners, so they steer clear of it. For Guerrillas, marketing has no mystique at all and is a whale of a lot of fun because they enjoy launching a marketing attack and knowing they'll succeed. Guerrillas know well what marketing is and they certainly know what marketing is not.

GUERRILLA EXERCISE:

Examine all of your past marketing efforts to determine which ones are real marketing and which ones are not. Begin concentrating on doing more of those which are marketing and eliminate those which are only pretenders.

Put a checkmark next to each marketing truism that characterizes your current marketing:

My marketing is not merely advertising.

My marketing is not merely direct mail.

My marketing is not merely telemarketing.

My marketing is not merely a brochure.

My marketing is not merely a yellow pages listing.

My marketing is not show business.

My marketing is not merely a stage for humor.

My cleverness does not get in the way of my message.

I do not consider marketing too complicated to control.

My marketing is more than merely having a website.

I do not expect miracles from my marketing.

GUERRILLA ACTION STEPS:

A. Circle each truism that does not have a checkmark.

B. List the action you will take, in the space provided, to earn a checkmark for each listed insight into marketing that you possess.

C. Execute your marketing in a way that reflects your insights, profiting by your understanding of what marketing is and is not.

DAVID L. HANCOCK

Guerrilla Marketing Myths

The path to entrepreneurial success is mined with booby traps disguised as words of wisdom. Guerrillas can distinguish the facts from the fables.

There are many marketing myths that ought to be tucked away where you keep the collected works of the Brothers Grimm, Aesop and Mother Goose. They may be fun to read, but they are disastrous to any marketing campaign. Heaven help us, there are hundreds of these myths circulating, but we'll deal only with ten of them here because if I wrote about all of them, your computer would probably crash while laughing in disbelief.

Myth: It's good to have a lot of white space in advertisements, brochures, and other printed material.

Truth: Your prospects and customers care a whole lot more about information than blank space. They want to know what your offering can do for them, not that you can afford to run a lot of white space. Usually white space substitutes for powerful ideas, a list of benefits and a fertile imagination. Attention should be drawn by substance, not emptiness. Yes, white space is aesthetically pleasing, but profits are even more delightful.

Myth: Use short copy because people just won't read long copy.

Truth: People real long books, long articles and long letters. They read whatever interests them, and the more they're interested, the more they'll read. If you give people more data than they need, they'll either buy from you or they won't buy. If you give them less, they won't buy – period. Studies show that readership of marketing materials falls off dramatically after the first 50 words, but stays high from 50 words to 500 words. That means your non-prospects will turn the page in a hurry, but your prospects will read and hang on to every word, trying to learn as much as they can.

Myth: It is costly to purchase television time.

Truth: This myth was once the truth, but cable and satellite TV have obliterated it. The cost to run a prime time commercial in any major market in the U.S. is now $20 or less, often as low as $5. Better still, cable TV allows you to cherry-pick where your commercials will run so that they air only in communities where your prospects live. You can advertise on CNN, MTV, ESPN, A&E, The Discovery Channel – any satellite-delivered programming. And cable companies will produce your spot for a cost near $1000, a far cry from the $197,000 average spent on production last year.

Myth: Sell the sizzle, not the steak.

Truth: The idea is to sell the solution, not the sizzle. The easiest way to sell anything is to position it as the solution to a problem. If you look for the sizzle and not the problem, you're looking in the wrong direction. Your prospects might appreciate the sizzle, but they'll write a check for the solution. Your job is to spot the problem then offer your product or service as the solution. If you think solutions, you'll market solutions. If you think sizzle, you'll sell sizzle. You'll find that the path of least resistance to the sale leads right through the problem to the solution.

Myth: Truly great marketing works instantly.

Truth: First-rate sales work instantly. Great limited-time offers work instantly. But great marketing is not made up of sales and limited-time offers alone. These will attract customers, but they won't be loyal and they'll be won by whoever offers the lowest price. Great marketing is made up of creating a desire for your offering in the minds of qualified prospects, then peppering your offers with sales and limited-time offers. But a program of fast-buck marketing usually leads to oblivion. The best marketing in America took a long time to establish itself. Just ask the Marlboro man. Or the Green Giant. Or that lonely Maytag repairman. None of that marketing worked instantly, but it has worked for decades and still does.

Myth: Marketing should entertain and amuse.

Truth: Show business should entertain and amuse. But marketing should sell your offering. This widespread myth is based upon studies that show people like marketing that entertains. They like it but they sure don't respond to it. Alas, the marketing community nurtures this myth by presenting awards based upon glitz and glitter, humor and originality, special effects and killer jingles. Those awards should be given for profit increases and nothing else. The only thing that should glitter should be your bottom line.

Myth: Marketing should be changed regularly to keep it fresh and new.

Truth: The longer that solid marketing promotes a product or service, the better. Guerrillas create marketing plans that can guide their efforts for five or ten years, even longer. How long have people been in good hands with Allstate? How long have Rice Krispies snapped, crackled and popped? Do you think these marketers would be more successful if they kept changing the marketing around to keep it fresh? I think not.

Myth: Marketing is successful if it is memorable.

Truth: Marketing is successful if it moves your product or service at a profit. Memorability has nothing to do with it. Whether people like it or not has nothing to do with it. Studies continue to prove that there is no relationship between remembering your marketing and buying your offering. All that matters is if people are motivated to make a purchase. So don't aim for Memorability as much as desirability because that leads to profitability.

Myth: Bad publicity is better than no publicity at all.

Truth: Bad publicity is bad for your business. No publicity is a lot healthier for you. People just love to gossip, especially about businesses that have done something so awful that the media exposes it. Guerrillas love publicity but avoid bad publicity because they know it spreads faster than wildfire.

Myth: All that really counts is earning a honest profit.

Truth: Good taste and sensitivity also count. Marketing, as part of mass communications, is part of the evolutionary process. It educates, informs, announces, enlightens and influences human behavior. Because it does, it has an obligation to offend nobody, to present its material with taste and decency, to be honest and to benefit customers. If it does that and earns profits too, it is true Guerrilla marketing.

GUERRILLA EXERCISE:

Notice the newspaper advertising, magazine ads, television spots, radio commercials direct mail, email, and websites designed to motivate you. Make a list of ten examples of this marketing that arises from people believing in the mythology of marketing. This will help you realize that as a Guerrilla, you will never run a mythological marketing campaign.

Make a checkmark by each of the myths that you do not believe:

It is good to have a lot of white space in marketing materials.

People do not read long copy.

It is very costly to purchase time on television.

Marketing should sell the sizzle and not the steak.

Good marketing works instantly.

Marketing is supposed to entertain and amuse.

Marketing should change regularly.

Marketing should be memorable above all else.

Bad publicity is better than no publicity.

The only purpose of marketing is to earn a profit.

GUERRILLA ACTION STEPS:

A. Circle each statement that does not have a checkmark.

B. List the action you will take to cease your belief in a myth. Your goal is a checkmark next to each myth.

C. Adjust your current marketing to reflect the truths of marketing and operate by none of the myths.

Guerrilla Marketing with Technology

The greatest boom to Guerrilla marketing has been the inexpensive, powerful and easy-to-use technology of today. I hate saying the word "empower," but technology definitely empowers a small business.

Up till a few years ago, technology was not associated with small business marketing. It was connected with databases, inventory control, electronic spreadsheets and word processing. It was complicated, costly – and its affect on small business didn't stretch into the arena of marketing.

But that was then.

Now, technology is in the process of revolutionizing small business, enabling many small business owners to dream new dreams, and then attain them in surprisingly brief time spans. Sure, technology helps all businesses in all ways. But it helps small businesses in the biggest ways.

For one thing, technology gives small businesses a blatantly unfair advantage because it allows them to look and act big without having to spend big. The price of credibility has dropped while credibility itself has become more precious. Technology provides small business owners with the tickets to credibility – season tickets – in fact, lifetime tickets.

Until recently, the advantages of small business over big business were gained by utilizing the weapons of personalized service, extra flexibility, and speed. Today, Guerrilla business owners, those who want conventional goals using unconventional means, have a secret weapon. That weapon blasts open the doors to increased profits.

The secret weapon is technology – though the secret is getting out as those who know it are unable to hide the grins on their faces. Technology is simpler than ever, so simple that high-tech is becoming easy-tech. It's so inexpensive that in 2000, you can invest a low four figure sum to purchase what in l982 took a mid six figure sum.

Technology has evened out the playing field, removed the dome from the top and opened the entire world to the entrepreneur. Online, that practitioner of free enterprise can connect with allies and customers anywhere in the community and on the planet. That small business owner has learned that virtual is a state of mind that means "connected." Being connected has never been so low in cost and high in value.

To many Guerrilla marketers, technology is to be lauded because it has put them online – giving them access to the speed of email, the power of fresh information, the warmth of closely connected people, and the marketing muscle of the World Wide Web. To others, technology is the hero because it allows them to flourish in a home-based business.

Examining just those areas where technology adds potency to marketing, I find 20 that are especially intriguing if you take seriously the business of earning consistent profits.

1. The first way is in the area of marketing online. A computer can help you design and then post your own website online. But before you rush off and do that, heed this: a website cannot help you unless you know marketing. It is a marketing medium, perhaps the best and most comprehensive ever – but it is not marketing all by itself and it is no guarantee of success. You must be an ace marketer in order to market online successfully. You've got to know how to market what you sell as well as marketing your

website. The moment you think of going online is when to start thinking of promoting your website offline. That process should never stop.

Marketing online doesn't merely mean the web. It means emailing, posting notices at forums, engaging in chats, doing research, gathering market data and having a website. The keys to succeeding online are in creating compelling content, changing that content regularly, responding at nearly the speed of light, and personalizing your messages. There may be 100 million people on the Internet but your prospects must feel you're talking to them one at a time.

I promised you 20 ways that technology helps you market and then I went off on a tangent because I want you to use technology the right way online. I also want you to be aware of 19 ways technology can help you offline:

2. Newsletters — Good ones are mailed to customers and prospects on a regular basis and follow the rule of 75-25.

3. Flyers — Distribute them in a variety of ways, as signs, in orders, to fusion marketing partners to distribute as you distribute theirs.

4. Direct mail letters — Have an inventory of proven letters in your computer, set to print, personalize and mail.

5. Postcards — They take away from the recipient the decision of whether or not to open the envelope.

6. Business cards — Include your name, company name, title, address, phone, fax number, email address, website, logo, tag line; your card may open up to reveal a list of benefits offered and services available.

7. Brochures — Perfect forums for including all the details; they should be offered for free in your other marketing and posted online.

8. Catalogs — You can increase revenues through catalogs, now easy and inexpensive to design and produce a potentially big profit-center.

9. Gift certificates — People are on the lookout for gift ideas and a gift certificate might be perfect. Mention them on signs, in brochures.

10. Coupons — Offer discounts, free merchandise, services, anything to intensify prospect's desire for your product. Coupons are very versatile.

11. Contest entry forms — Smart small businesses hold contests in order to get names for their mailing lists.

12. Club ID cards — Form a frequent buyer club or VIP customer club: sealing your relationship with the customers with an attractive ID card.

13. Signs — Because so many towns have community bulletin boards, Guerrillas are sure to post their signs on those boards. Guerrillas know that computers can transform some signs into posters.

14. Point-of-purchase materials — Guerrillas produce POP materials that tie in with their other marketing. Their computers do the hard work.

15. Trade show materials — You can produce compelling graphic presentations of sales stories strictly for use at trade shows.

16. Flipcharts — Audio-visual aids are built-in and your sales story has an order and flow. These can be portable, economical, and flexible.

17. Books — Technology helps Guerrillas from producing labels and tags to publishing their own books, proving they're the experts.

18. Invitations — Guerrillas print formal invitations to customers to private sales, parties and special events. They always play favorites.

19. Proposals — Computer-designed proposals add credibility, visibility, and excitability while instilling confidence in you beyond any price tag.

20. Multi-media presentations — These once complex and now simple forums let you demonstrate your benefits with extraordinary impact.

Technology lets small business gain credibility and provide speed and power in an age when credibility is crucial, speed is revered and power comes from being part of a team. Speed comes from cellular, wireless, pager, fax, email, and voicemail technology. Power comes from networking and sharing technology.

If you're Guerrilla marketing with technology, you're headed in the right direction. If you're Guerrilla marketing without technology, you're not really Guerrilla marketing at all.

GUERRILLA EXERCISE:

Make three lists now. The first should contain the technology you are using right now. The second should contain the technology you'll be using within two years. The third should contain the technology that your customers use. The closer the third list is to your first list and second list, the better you are marketing properly with technology.

Put a checkmark next to each of the technologies you currently employ:

Fax machine

Voice mail

Pager

Cell phone

Computer

High speed Internet access

Wireless technology

Two-way radio

CD-ROM

Palm Pilot

GUERRILLA ACTION STEPS:

A. Circle each technology your business currently lacks.

B. Determine whether an investment in each technology you are not employing will increase your overall profitability.

C. Write a list of which missing technology you will acquire and the month and year you will acquire it. The goal is to have technology that matches that of your customers and that earns profits for your business.

DAVID L. HANCOCK

Guerrilla Tickets to Ride to Success

This is a whole new ballgame and your tickets to the old ballgame won't get you very good seats.

Riding the Guerrilla marketing train requires you to reexamine the baggage you'll bring along. In the area of marketing, you'll certainly have to leave behind a lot of old ideas and myths, notions and traditions. But you surely want to take with you at least the five essential tickets to ride with confidence in your success.

Guerrillas enter success with momentum because they have those tickets. They know exactly where they're heading and they have the right tickets to their destinations. To generate and capitalize upon your own momentum, to travel first-class into the future, it makes sense for you to learn the five destinations of the Guerrilla and their five tickets to ride. You can go to the same destinations; you can have the same tickets:

1. The first is your Identity Ticket. It's the ticket that leads to close relationships. You get it with consistent and never-ending follow-up. You stay in touch with your customers and key prospects so regularly that you become part of their identity, someone they trust, someone they refer to their friends and associates. You convey your own identity in all of your marketing to them so they know clearly who you are and why you're good. Because you know

that marketers either follow-up forever or fail, follow-up is your middle name. I can read it there on your Identity Ticket.

2. The second is your Humanity Ticket. Whatever new and brilliant technologies you select to energize your company in the marketing arena, you always remember that your customers and prospects are people first, every one of them unique and special. So your marketing messages to them are warm and human, attentive to details of their lives, caring of their progress, helpful and informative, personalized whenever possible. This ticket leads to bonding and loyalty, far in excess of that enjoyed by most small business owners. Customer research questionnaires provide the information Guerrillas need to prove their humanity. It's vital in an increasingly impersonal society.

3. The third is your History Ticket. Lots of new and start-up companies have no histories. You do and your ticket leads to credibility. The more you have, the easier it is to buy from you. Your history ticket is dated from the day you launched your business, includes your marketing strategy, your list of satisfied customers, your past success stories, your past publicity reprints, everything you've done to earn the confidence of your market. That History Ticket, probably presented on your website, in your brochure, in your mailings, in your ads, will bypass the skepticism that faces new businesses and pave the way to future sales with trust.

4. The fourth is your Technology Ticket. Of course, you've conquered all traces of technophobia and now use technology to help you serve customers, scout for new prospects and link with fusion marketing partners, research the competition and create a plethora of marketing materials for

yourself. This ticket leads to professionalism, but it has side tracks that lead to places you don't really want to do. Many lead to an over-reliance on what technology can do rather than what it can do for you. Some side tracks lead you to glamour and hype instead of useful information, others to glitz and flash that your website visitors don't want to see, still others to fill your TV and print ads with special effects instead of reasons to want what you offer. Guerrillas stay on the right track with their technology, using it as a guide and not as a master.

5. The fifth ticket is your Action Ticket. It leads to accomplishment instead of conversation. That ticket is where you find your roadmap in the form of your marketing calendar. It's where you can see the specific tasks you must perform so as to keep your marketing in constant action, to keep your name at the forefront of your market's awareness. The other tickets are worthless unless your Action Ticket is put to full use. Marketing is something that many people discuss and analyze, but Guerrillas view it as a time and opportunity to take action, to do something, to capitalize upon the momentum they've achieved to go soaring into success, not missing a beat.

These five tickets are yours if you have the awareness of their importance, the desire to reach their destinations, and the attitude to use them with enthusiasm. With that awareness, desire and attitude, you're well-equipped to enter a new century with exactly what you need for profits, control and certainty.

GUERRILLA EXERCISE:

You saw this one coming. Determine which of the five tickets you already hold, and then determine which ones you'll need, then do all it takes to get them. Without them, we both know you're in a river and you don't have a paddle.

Place a checkmark next to each of the tickets you already hold:

An identity ticket

A humanity ticket

A history ticket

A technology ticket

An action ticket

GUERRILLA ACTION STEPS:

A. Circle each ticket that does not have a checkmark next to it.

B. State the action you will take to earn this ticket, using the space beneath each ticket.

C. Take each action you have listed so that you hold all five tickets.

DAVID L. HANCOCK

The Importance of Permission

With so much interruption marketing going on these days, the way to succeed is to gain permission to market to people. Once you have it, you're in clover. Without it, you're in trouble.

Sometimes the student becomes the teacher. That's exactly what happened to Jay Conrad Levinson when Seth Godin, co-author of three books with him, authored his own "Permission Marketing: Turning Strangers into Friends and Friends into Customers." It changed his entire outlook about marketing and can dramatically change the beauty of your bottom line.

Seth, once a student of Jay Conrad Levinson's, now has enlightened him to the presence of two kind of marketing in the world today. The first, most common, most expensive, most ineffective and most old-fashioned, is interruption marketing. That's when marketing such as a TV commercial, radio spot, magazine or newspaper ad, telemarketing call, or direct mail letter interrupts whatever you're doing to state its message. Most people pay very little attention to it, now more than ever because there is so much of it and because many minds now unconsciously filter it out.

The opposite of interruption marketing is the newest, least expensive, and most effective kind. It's called permission marketing – because prospects give their permission for you to market to them.

It works like this. You offer your prospects an enticement to volunteer to pay attention to your marketing. The enticement may be a prize for playing a game. It could be information prospects consider to be valuable. It might be a discount coupon. Perhaps it's membership to a privileged group such as a frequent buyer club, a birthday club. Maybe it's entry into a sweepstakes. And it might even take the form of an actual free gift. All you ask in return is permission to market to these people. Nothing else.

Alas, you'll have to use interruption marketing in order to secure that important permission. And you'll have to track your costs like crazy, figuring how much it costs you to gain each permission – easily figured by analyzing your media costs divided by number of permissions granted.

Once you've embarked upon a permission marketing campaign, you can spend less time marketing to strangers and more time marketing to friends. You can move your marketing from beyond mere reach and frequency and into the realm of trust.

Once you've obtained permission from your prospects, your marketing will take on three exciting characteristics. It will be anticipated, meaning people will actually look forward to hearing from you. It will be personal, meaning the messages are directly related to the prospect. And it will be relevant, meaning you know for sure that the marketing is about something in which the prospect is interested.

Permission marketing is not about share of market, not even about share of mind. Instead, it's about share of wallet. You find as many new actual customers as you can, then extract the maximum value from each customer. You convert the largest number of prospects into customers, using your invaluable permission to accomplish this. You focus your marketing only on prospects and not on the world at large.

Let's use an existing mortgage shop as an example of permission marketing in action. This shop uses interruption marketing to run ads at home expos and in magazines that feature other ads from home expos. But the ads do not attempt to sell their services. Instead, they focus solely upon motivating prospects to send for a video and a brochure, upon securing their permission to accept your marketing with an open mind.

Once the prospects receive the video, they soon see that it, too, does not try to sell the mortgage services. It is geared only to get permission to set up a meeting. But having seen a video of the shop facilities, activities, happy customers and attentive staff, the prospect is all set to say yes to a personal meeting.

At the in-person meeting, the sale is closed. And once a customer closes the loan, chances are pretty darned good he or she will not only stay loyal for several more transactions, but also will refer a brother, a sister, a cousin, a colleague or a friend – or all of these.

Notice that the only goal of each step is to expand permission for you to take another step rather than making the ultimate sale. Who uses permission marketing these days? Record clubs. Book clubs. Marketers who offer a free brochure. Even my own website at www.davidlhancock.com offers a weekly marketing message for only $3 per year – in affect, gaining permission to market to all those who sign up.

The biggest boon to permission marketing is the internet — but only by those who treat it as an interactive medium and not like TV. As clutter becomes worse, permission becomes more valuable. The moral: since only a limited number of companies within a market niche can secure permission, get moving on your own permission marketing program pronto.

GUERRILLA EXERCISE:

Make a list of the methods you'll use to gain permission, then what marketing materials you'll use once you have that permission.

Make a checkmark next to each marketing weapon you use in order to gain consent to send more marketing materials:

Newspapers	Radio
Television	Magazine ads
Newspaper ads	Direct mail letters
Direct mail postcards	Postcard deck
Telemarketing Website	Email
Trade shows	Brochures
Seminars	Yellow pages ads
Classified ads	Movie ads

Now, put a checkmark next to each item you offer in order to broaden your consent:

Brochure	Website
Free consultation	Video
Audiotape	Demonstration
Free estimate	Free gift
Newsletter	E-zine
Catalog	Poster

GUERRILLA ACTION STEPS:

A. Circle each weapon you are not using to gain or broaden consent from your prospects to receive marketing materials.

B. Make a list of the actions you will take to employ each weapon and the month and year you will begin to employ it.

C. Activate each weapon, one by one, so as to gain consent from all of your prospective customers.

DAVID L. HANCOCK

Guerrilla Marketing as a Mating Ritual

I f you view marketing as one big and profitable mating ritual, you'll be viewing it in exactly the right way.

The whole idea of Guerrilla marketing is to transform cold prospects into consenting partners. As with superb sex, marketers shouldn't be in a hurry, shouldn't direct their energies to disinterested people and must realize that the consummation of a loving relationship won't take place without proper wooing, without knowing exactly what turns on the prospect.

When small business owners think less of marketing as impersonal communications and more as sexual journey, they will be far more able to market with success. In today's cluttered environment of marketing, Instead of pondering numbers and demographics, explore instead the concepts of romance and love.

That means realizing that falling in love with the right person and keeping the relationship delicious and satisfying is not so much a single major event as a step-by-step process. It begins by playing the field and determining just who you want to date in the first place. During this step, Guerrilla marketers concentrate upon the compatibility factor. They keep their radar attuned to the proper chemistry that leads to mutual understanding and eventual consent. Unfazed by superficial allure, they seek soul mates more than customers. Their taste and discretion helps reduce their marketing costs because their targets reflect quality over quantity.

Their next step is gaining un-carnal knowledge. They seek information about prospects who have caught their fancy so they can satisfy their needs more than their wants – because Guerrillas realize people often want what they don't need, and providing it is hardly the basis of a long term relationship. They seek shared values in customers as they would in lovers, gaining information as they impart information, much in the manner of two people getting to know each other – with romance on their mind. They treat all prospects differently, just as they want to be treated. They learn those ways with research and two-way communication.

It's at this point that Guerrillas engage in flirting — taking that first step towards gaining consent. Marketing with personalized messages, treating advertising not as the way to make the sale but as first step in gaining consent, they become attractive to those who have attracted them.

When the courtship begins, Guerrillas pay very close attention and prove that they care. They enter into dialogues with those for whom they are lusting and know what to say for that lust to be returned. Any courtship is intensified with gifts of love, and it is no different in the Guerrilla marketer's search for consenting partners. Gifts can be gift-wrapped or come in the form of prizes, memberships in loyalty groups, newsletters, booklets, regular email updates. Each prospect knows that their individuality is recognized.

Next comes making out, connecting even closer with prospects by becoming more intimate in marketing. By listening carefully to learn of likes and dislikes, specific problems, Guerrillas learn to make promises they can keep. Their penchant for taking action broadens even more the consent for which they strive.

The step in marketing that most relates to foreplay is when marketers give to their partners the exact pleasure that they want. They capitalize upon the interactivity afforded by online communications to become a part of their prospect's identities. They customize their messages to each prospect, not only making them feel special but proving their devotion.

Guerrilla marketers and their prospects achieve consummation by closing the sale with mutual consent. Rather than having rushed, their timing is impeccable and their fulfillment implies a commitment. The marketer has consistently demonstrated empathy for the partner – with the goal of providing joy and satisfaction. The earth may not tremble, but a lasting bond has been created.

During the afterglow, the connection is solidified. This is accomplished with assiduous follow-up – proving in a way that the marketer still respects the prospect in the morning. Statements of warm appreciation are made resulting in prospects who are so delighted they just cannot help but relate their joy to other people they know.

The entire process involves a lot more than a mere sexual dalliance but is the start of a long and happy marriage. The devotion of the small business owner is unmistakable because it builds upon details that have been learned, specific tastes of each customer and their shared experience of sale, purchase and use.

The more you view the marketing process as a mating ritual more than an economic ritual, the longer will be your list of consenting and delighted partners.

GUERRILLA EXERCISE:

Make a list of your hottest prospects, no pun intended, then determine at which stage of the courtship process you are with each of them. Then, you'll know what to do next. All lovers are not created equal. Guerrillas have far more sex appeal.

Place a checkmark next to each of the mating rituals that you follow in marketing your business:

Playing the field

Gaining un-carnal knowledge

Flirting

Courtship

Making out

Foreplay

Consummation

Afterglow

Marriage

GUERRILLA ACTION STEPS:

A. Circle each stage of the mating ritual that you do not employ in marketing your business.

B. Make a list of those rituals.

C. Create the marketing materials you do not use so that you are prepared to carry out the entire marketing/mating ritual. A long and happy marriage comes only after you have taken all the steps to make your customer/partner feel romanced and satisfied.

DAVID L. HANCOCK

Guerrilla Marketing the Closing

Now we are going to get specific, mortgage specific. Sit back relax, grab your Mountain Dew™ and open your mind. No I'm not going to fill it with off the wall concepts or vague ideas just as an add-on; I'm going to give you instructions that you can measurably see results right now! Hang On!

Close the Closing

What? Stay with me here. Close the Closing means just that. If you are not already attending each and every closing you are loosing 70% of your earned referrals! No kidding, 70%!

You've already invested in the client, gotten to know them and hopefully built a rapport with them; why not see them through! Most mortgage consultants are afraid to go in case something comes up, or because the process had some bumps in it.

HELLO! That is why YOU need to be there! Would you like to have an uninformed closing agent (or worse yet a hostile agent) talk a little too much. Here is an example: Let's say my client had a less than perfect credit history. So their rate was slightly higher than market. Not too far fetched, but higher. And of course less than perfect credit history usually means slightly higher fees as well.

My client wanted to select their own attorney, so we lost a little control there. When the attorney opened the package to start the closing his first words were "Look at this, this rate it is higher than market right now, and why are you being charged these fees..." I kid you not!

Fortunately, after building a rock solid foundation with the client, they spoke up and defended the loan for me (rare). They indicated that they knew what they were getting and why their situation deemed it necessary, and that I had committed to staying in contact with them by periodically reviewing their situation in hopes to improve the situation as soon as possible (there is another bonus secret there).

Go to every closing that is physically possible. No one else seems to be doing this, or at least very few. So few in fact that when you do show up, everyone either acts surprised or goes on about how special the client is that the lender came to see it through.

Now I hope your mouth is watering, because you will be able to look back in time and see the very day you started doing this, because your client will appreciate it and tell others. The attorney or closing agent will see and eventually appreciate you being there that they will refer clients to you. And so on...

Can you imagine taking a new direction where you actually refer clients to your real estate agents? Or better yet, refer new clients to real estate agents that you want to become part of you network!

Guerrilla Marketing the Flip Side

If you're committed to your success, this book filled with tips, strategies, tools and concepts will definitely be an asset for you and your business. But if you truly want to take your business to the next level listen to this. Oh, by the way, I hope you are still sitting down, because this is even more powerful, more "why didn't I think of that" than Closing the Closing!

Market the Flip Side

That's right! Market the Flip Side! You've already spent time and money with the current client and agent; why not realize triple the response on that effort?

This is part of my "Guerrilla Marketing" but here is basically what you need to do: Most real estate purchase transactions, the core of your business, have agents and sellers, correct. Those interested parties to your transaction need to know who you are! Remember earlier secrets to be unique? Well, day one on your next purchase transaction starts with marketing the flip side.

Now don't make the mistake of trying to sell the other agent or the sellers. Be stealthy; make them *want* to do business with you because they *have* to. Because they *need* to have the superior lender support like you are giving the buyer.

Contact the seller and listing agent via letter or phone call to introduce yourself and let them know you will be keeping them informed with the progress. Open the doors of communication, invite questions keep them up to date. This way you remain in control of the transaction and impress everyone involved.

You will eventually need to hire an assistant because your business will be growing exponentially.

Todd Duncan from The Duncan Group said: "If you don't have an assistant, you are one". So true.

Guerrilla Marketing
In Tough Times: Part I

It's ironic to be writing a book about "tough times" during one of our best and longest real estate booms we've hade in 10 years.

Well, I'll let you in on a little secret. I didn't really write this because I thought there was a need for some magic formula to help you survive impending tough times... I wrote this because YOU think you need one.

The truth is, sometimes thinking times are tough are what make them so.

Yes, we need to give a nod of acknowledgement to tough times, and perhaps even adjust the way we operate to a small extent, but only that. That nod we give needs to be a careful and suspicious one. Nodding too hard at tough times will stop you in your tracks fast.

I've had a few rough months here and there when so-called recessions were in full swing, but I never let anyone in my office say the R word. Use of that word was strictly forbidden. Here's why...

What it comes down to is, when we analyzed the tough months, we discovered that what really prevented us from doing well was ourselves. We had technical and management issues that prevented us from performing as well as we would have liked.

How easy it would have been to blame our poor performance on the recession! It's the easy way out, and every fiber of our being was screaming to say it.

But we didn't — and it made all the difference. We're stronger and tougher now that we've looked internally for improvement and not externally. It would have been so comfortable and so easy to wallow in self-pity and talk longingly of the "good ole days" when life was so much easier.

Ultimately a recession becomes an excuse for laziness and the patch over our shortcomings. The media starts this lie and the lazy nature in us all perpetuates it.

The real antidote for tough times is an iron will and a good stiff belt of old fashioned common sense. When it comes to marketing common sense, "Guerrilla Marketing" is the backbone of marketing wisdom. It doesn't get much stiffer or to the point — and it gets the job done like none other.

So, if you feel like you've heard some of this before, stop yourself right there. Don't dismiss it — hear it. Hear it like you've never heard it before. Because that message, my friend, *IS* the antidote for tough times. You just need to digest it.

Tough Times Don't Have To Be As Tough As You Think

In every down economy, some businesses lose money while others seemingly coin money. This chapter is designed to put you into the latter category. The plain fact is that Guerrillas have an advantage during tough times. They are able to work in relatively shorter time frames. Their desire for information enables them to market more quickly and creatively to market needs.

The Guerrilla lives by different rules during tough times than during boom times. The Guerrilla attacks when the competition retreats and the attacks are concentrated where the Guerrilla offers specific product or service advantages. Retreating companies leave voids in the market, ideal niches for Guerrilla mortgage brokers.

Guerrillas do not commit all their resources to any one front because they try to maintain resources for new options and for potential confrontations with the competition. Flexibility is an asset. Successful Guerrilla Mortgage Brokers try to be inconspicuous about their success, reducing the chances of being copied when attacked by their competitors.

They know many companies have scrubbed or reduced their marketing budgets to combat tough times and that it will cost those firms three dollars for every dollar formerly spent to reach the same level of consumer recognition and share of mind they previously enjoyed.

Guerrillas are aware that their prospects are more likely to recall marketing messages delivered consistently during a fragile economy, even if they are smaller and less frequently delivered. So they maintain the attitude of a Guerrilla even when the economic situation is in its darkest days.

"In a dog-eat-dog economy, the Doberman is boss," said Edward Abbey, the author and naturalist. In this regard, the Doberman and the Guerrilla have a lot in common.

Guerrillas know that they must seek profits from their current customers. They drink at the fountain of customer follow-up. They are world-class experts at getting their customers to expand the size of their purchase. Because the cost of selling to a brand-new customer is six times higher than selling to an existing customer, Guerrilla marketers turn their gaze from strangers to friends.

This reduces the cost of marketing while reinforcing the customer relationship. To Guerrillas, follow-up means marketing to some of the most cherished citizens of planet Earth — their customers.

When your customers are confronted with their daily blizzard of junk mail and unwanted email, your mailing piece won't be scrapped with the others, and your email won't be instantly deleted. After all, these folks know you. They identify with you. They trust you. They know you stay in touch with them for a reason. So they'll be delighted to purchase — or at least check out — that new product or service they didn't know you offered. They'll always be inclined to buy from a company they've patronized instead of experimenting with a company that has not yet won a share of their mind.

When you follow up with intensity, it proves that you really care and that you'll be there when the customer truly needs you. If you haven't started a customer-stroking program yet, start it tomorrow. And whatever you do, put it in writing and determine two things: who will take the responsibility for each follow-up activity, and when that activity will take place.

In any rugged economy, the telephone is a remarkably effective follow-up weapon for Guerrillas. You certainly don't have to use the phone to follow up all of your mailings to customers, but research proves that it always will boost your sales and profits. Sure, telephone follow-up is a tough task. But it works. Anyhow, no one ever said that Guerrilla Marketing is a piece of cake.

Email ranks up there with the telephone, possibly even outranks it. It's inexpensive. It's fast. It lets you prove you care. It helps strengthen your relationship. And in your subject line, you can mention the recession if your offering is in any way related to it.

Lean upon your website as well. Instead of telling your whole story with other marketing, use that other marketing to direct people to your site. Then, use the site to give a lot of information and advance the sale to consummation.

Guerrillas are able to think of additional products and services that can establish new sources of profits for them. In any kind of economy, they are on the alert for strategic alliances — fusion marketing efforts with others. This kind of cooperative marketing makes sense at all times, but makes the most sense during tough times, when companies must market aggressively while reducing their marketing investment.

Guerrilla Mortgage Brokers cease most *broadcasting* and increase their *narrow-casting* to customers and carefully targeted prospects. A faltering economy is tough. Still, when the going gets tough, Guerrillas make sizeable bank deposits. Many see beauty in economic ugliness.

In gloomy economic days, when everything else seems to be shrinking, think in terms of expanding your offerings. Do absolutely everything you can to motivate customers to expand the size of their purchase. Prove that buying right now is a wise move *because of* the tough times.

In marketing to customers and to non-customers show that you are fully aware of the economic situation and that you have priced your services accordingly. Even though your marketing is always truthful, exert even more of an effort during bad times to make it sound even more truthful. Candid language is a powerful weapon. Admit that times are tough; admit that people must be extra careful when buying things; explain that you're fully aware of the economy and have taken special steps because of it.

This chapter will help you investigate a treasure-trove of marketing tactics that can help you weather the toughest of times. But learning about them is only half the battle. It's when you begin putting them into practice you'll assure that the real tough times are those faced by your competition.

GUERRILLA EXERCISE:

Ask yourself 10 easy questions:

1. Am I attacking or retreating on the marketing front?

2. Am I marketing with more than one marketing weapon?

3. Is my marketing exposed to my target market consistently?

4. Are some of my marketing funds directed at current customers?

5. Am I making use of the telephone in my marketing?

6. Do I take advantage of marketing with email?

7. Is my website working to advance my marketing thrust?

8. Do I have any strategic alliances with other companies?

9. Do I automatically try to enlarge the size of each transaction?

10. Does my marketing admit that times are tough?

THE MORE YOU ANSWERED "YES" TO THESE QUESTIONS, THE MORE PRIMED YOU ARE TO MARKET IN TOUGH TIMES.

GUERRILLA ACTION STEPS:

A. Spend one hour examining the websites of your competition. Compare them with your own site and determine three ways you can improve your site.

B. Study today's newspaper to see what kinds tactics other types of companies are using to combat a down economy. Put into writing at least three of these tactics.

C. Make a list of the marketing efforts you are using specifically to combat the economic slowdown. The longer your list, the better.

DAVID L. HANCOCK

Guerrilla Marketing In Tough Times: Part II

The Importance Of Stressing Value

Whatever you do, don't make the mistake of thinking that the right price for tough times is the lowest price. Price becomes secondary during hard times; people are searching for value. If you offer customers great values — in the form of more flexible products, more encompassing services, or long-term economy — you'll earn higher profits than if you target your marketing solely to skinflints.

Tough times require superb values. And that's what Guerrillas offer. If you're truly a Guerrilla, you'll also eliminate any perceived risk of buying from you by stressing your money-back guarantee, your liberal guarantee and your deep commitment to service. Mention the names of others who have purchased from you.

Do you sell a high-priced product or service? It seems that a high price will be detrimental to you during challenging times. But just the opposite is true. If you offer high-priced items, use those tough times as a selling tool. Explain to people that during a rugged economy, it is crucial not to waste money. Therefore, they should protect their money by spending it wisely and not making a mistake. Mistakes can be financial disasters during a down economy. Makes sense, doesn't it?

Still, in any economic situation, every Guerrilla knows that the number one factor influencing purchase decisions is confidence. And the road to confidence is paved with credibility.

Having the lowest price won't help you much if your prospect doesn't trust you in the first place. Offering the widest selection and the most convenience won't aid your cause if your prospect thinks you're a crook.

You've got to face up to the glaring reality that prospects won't call your toll-free number, access your website, mail your coupon, come into your shop, visit your trade show booth, talk to your loan officers, talk to you on the phone, or even accept your generous freebie if they aren't confident in your company.

Time zips on by. Your prospects can't afford to waste it or their money with Mortgage Brokers that haven't earned their confidence. In order to earn that confidence — no stroll in the park, as you've most likely learned — you've got to use specific Guerrilla Marketing weapons and use them properly. I emphasize "properly" because even a smart bomb isn't a valuable weapon if it lands on your foot.

Guerrillas think in terms of getting down to the business of achieving and deserving credibility. All their marketing materials, whatever they say or show with their main message, also carry a "meta-message" — an unstated, yet powerful communiqué to prospects. The meta-message for 123 Mortgage of a superbly written direct mail letter on very inexpensive stationery is going to be quite different from the meta-message of the same letter for ABC Mortgage on costly stationery that looks and feels exquisite.

The paper stock carries a strong meta-message. So does the real or metered stamp. The typeface speaks volumes and the printed — or handwritten — signature is even more eloquent. The ABC Mortgage letter has superb stock, a clear and elegant typeface and a hand-signed signature, using blue ink and a fountain pen. These are tiny details. Tiny but nuclear-powered. Why? Credibility is why.

Not surprisingly, the 123 Mortgage letter, even though worded exactly like the ABC Mortgage letter, will not draw as healthy a response because of its weak meta-message. A powerful meta-message inspires confidence.

Entire marketing plans fall by the wayside because inattention to seemingly unimportant details undermines the prospect's confidence — even if that confidence was earned elsewhere. An amateurish logo or meme makes your company seem like an amateur. Any hint of amateurism in your marketing indicates to your prospects the potential for amateurism elsewhere in your company — throughout your company.

Does this mean that cheap stationery, a plain Jane website, fuzzy type, and poor English destroy your credibility? Not entirely. But shabbiness in these areas certainly do not contribute to your credibility.

Absolutely everything you do that is called marketing influences your credibility. The influence will be positive or negative, depending upon your taste, intelligence, sensitivity, and awareness of this power.

Be aware of it the moment you start operating your business, and if not then, right now. Begin the quest with the name of your company, your logo, your theme line, location, stationery, business card, package, brochure, business forms, interior decor, website, fusion marketing partners, even the attire worn by you and your people.

Communicate even more credibility with the building you're in, the people you employ, the technology you use, the follow-up in which you engage, the attention you pay to customers, the testimonials you display, your trade show booth, your signs, and surely the neatness of your premises.

The way your phones are answered can gain or lose credibility for you. Just yesterday, I decided not to make an expensive purchase from a store I had called simply because they put me on telephone hold for too long. Minor detail? Maybe, but somebody else now has my deposit check.

You gain credibility with your advertisements, listings in directories, columns and articles you write, books you publish, and talks you give. You gain it with your newsletter. You gain even more by your support of a noble cause such as the environment. All these little things add up to something called your reputation. The most important word in marketing — commitment — is something that also fuels your credibility. When people see that you are maintaining consistency in your marketing, especially during tough times, they'll assume you're just as committed to quality and service — and can deliver on them regardless of the economy.

All of your weapons must communicate the same meta-message — one that fits in with everything else in your marketing and with the reality of your offerings.

Credibility is not automatic but it is do-able. Give a seminar. Work hard for a community organization. Nudge customers into referring your business. Word-of-mouth is omnipotent in the credibility quest. The idea is for you to establish your expertise, your authority, your integrity, your conscientiousness, your professionalism, and therefore — your credibility.

When that PR person gets you into the newspaper, make reprints of the article and frame them, include them on your website, into your brochure, pop them into your newsletter, put them on your reception counter, stick them in your shop window. Cost? A bit of time. Result? A lot of credibility.

Trade shows can enhance your credibility and so can free workshops. Free consultations can do wonders for it and so can free credit reports or appraisals. Do glitz and glamour enhance your credibility? They do — but be careful that you don't send out the wrong message. If you're a discounter, glitz can sabotage your identity.

Want a shortcut to credibility? Run a full-page ad in a regional edition of a national magazine. Just running the ad won't net much credibility for you, but the reprints you display, mail, incorporate into other marketing, and proudly disseminate will. They'll all proclaim "As advertised in Time magazine." And if they don't say Time, they'll say some other prestigious publication.

All the credibility that millions of readers attach to the magazine — they suddenly attach to you. I'm not talking zillions of dollars here. I'm talking of a few thousand — and just one time. It's a small price to pay for credibility. You can get details about incredibly low costs for incredibly credible magazines by getting the free media kit from Media Networks, Inc. at 1-800-225-3457 or www.mni.com.

During a shaky economy, people are attracted to solid businesses. You can prove your stability by consistently stating your message and by remembering that credibility equates with profitability.

GUERRILLA EXERCISE:

1. Are all of your marketing messages emphasizing value?

2. Do you offer a long guarantee?

3. Can you use your price, high or low, as a selling tool?

4. Have you taken concrete steps to enhance your credibility?

5. Are you aware of the meta-message conveyed by your marketing?

ONCE AGAIN, EACH "YES" ANSWER POSITIONS YOUR COMPANY TO THRIVE DURING TOUGH TIMES.

GUERRILLA ACTION STEPS:

A. List five things you are doing now to earn extra consumer confidence and credibility.

B. List five additional things you can and will do to earn even more confidence and credibility.

C. Put into writing exactly why your offerings provide exceptional value.

DAVID L. HANCOCK

Guerrilla Marketing
In Tough Times: Part III

Using Consent Marketing Now More Than Ever

In addition to your consent marketing program, you've also got to realize that all customers are not created equal. Your "A" list customers spend more, buy more frequently, refer your business to others, happily complete customer questionnaires, give you names for your referral list, and are pleasant people overall.

Your "B" list customers buy from you, but aren't necessarily bright spots on your customer list. Your job as a Guerrilla is to treat both of these groups of customers very well. You must treat those "B" list customers like royalty — because that's what they expect and that's what they deserve.

You should treat your "A" list customers like family — because they are more profitable to your company and they help you maintain your sanity. A few months ago, my parents and I ate at a restaurant we've frequently visited. When presented with our check, we were given a fifteen percent discount along with a VIP card that would give us fifteen percent off on all future meals. The manager said, "You're very valued customers to us and this card is to show our appreciation."

Have we eaten there many times since? Have we recommended the restaurant to our friends? You know that the answers are a resounding "yes," and you can just imagine how we feel about that restaurant. But it doesn't take a discount to show your gratitude to your best customers. Just treating them extra-special and acknowledging that you appreciate their business is usually enough. Still, they do deserve special treatment.

During tough times, it doesn't cost you one extra cent to render extra superlative service, but you can be sure that your customers notice it. Your "A" list customers should receive advance notices of new products or services that you offer, of information that can help them succeed at their own goals.

Just think of the attention and kindness that you give to your friends. They appreciate you for it and happily return your friendship. Then think of the extra attention you probably lavish upon members of your own family. It's usually more than you give to your friends — not a whole lot more, but enough so that they feel like family. This is how it should be with your "A" list and "B" list customers.

Life is not always simple black and white. There are also many gray areas. If you're not certain whether a customer should be on your "A" list or "B" list, it's best to error on the side of caution and treat them as though they are members of your family.

GUERRILLA EXERCISE:

1. Go over your customer list and try to identify your "A" list and "B" list customers. This will take a bit of your time, but it will be worth the investment.

2. Consider actually "firing" some of your customers -- those who take up the most time, have the most problems, and do not prove their loyalty to you. Firing a customer is never fun, but it is worth your time — especially during a down economy.

GUERRILLA ACTION STEPS:

A. Put into writing a list of the things you do to treat your "B" list customers like royalty.

B. Put into writing a list of the things you do to treat your "A" list customers like family.

C. Formalize a program where your "A" list customers realize that you actually do give them special treatment.

Guerrilla Marketing
In Tough Times: Part IV

Free And Almost Free Marketing

Some kinds of marketing are very expensive. Other kinds are relatively inexpensive. This section is about marketing that is free or nearly free. Of the many kinds of free marketing, such as publicity or word-of-mouth, we'll concentrate here upon two types of free or nearly-free marketing:

1. Enlarging the size of each transaction — free

2. Going after repeat sales — nearly free

The first, enlarging the size of each transaction, costs you absolutely nothing. The customer has already decided to make a purchase from you. And all you've got to do is make it a larger purchase. You can do that by offering a service as part of a package, or by turning the single purchase into some kind of bundled offering. That means if a person hires you to finance their new home purchase, you say, "I can give you a very special price if you sign up for a Home Equity Line of Credit as well."

The cost to enlarge the transaction is zilch. Customers don't become offended when you make the offer. Instead, many of them appreciate it. A bookseller decided to put three books, all related, into a wicker gift basket. If a person was interested in one of them, the bookseller would point out the gift basket. Very often, the person would buy the whole package, tripling the size of the transaction. The cost of marketing the package was zero.

You can be certain that car dealers, such as BMW, provide a lot of upgrade training to their sales staffs. A person drives to a BMW showroom with the idea of buying the least expensive model. But that's probably not going to happen — due to that upgrade training. Upgrading the size of a transaction is simple because the person has already decided to buy from you.

Your job now is to come up with package offers. Perhaps you can even link up with one of your fusion marketing partners — and make a "commission" on each sale for which you're responsible. Again, that represents no cost to you.

Repeat sales is a method of nearly free marketing — one with a payoff very disproportionate to your investment. Why do you suppose most businesses lose customers? Poor service? Nope. Poor quality? Nope. Well, then why? Apathy after the sale. Most businesses lose customers by ignoring them to death. A numbing 68 percent of all business lost in America is lost due to apathy after the sale.

Misguided Mortgage Brokers think that marketing is over once they've closed the loan. WRONG! WRONG! WRONG! Marketing only just begins once you've closed the loan. It's of momentous importance to you and your company that you understand this. I'm sure you will by the time you've come to the end of this section.

First of all, understand how Guerrillas view follow up. They make it part of their DNA because they know it now costs six times more to sell something to a new customer than to an existing customer. When a Guerrilla closes a loan, the customer receives a follow-up thank-you note within 48 hours. When's the last time a business sent you a thank-you note within 48 hours? Maybe once? Maybe never? Probably never.

The Guerrilla sends another note or perhaps makes a phone call 30 days after the closing. This contact is to see if everything is going all right with the loan and if the customer has any questions. It is also to help solidify the relationship. The what? The relationship. Guerrillas know that the way to develop relationships, the key to survival in an increasingly entrepreneurial society, is through assiduous customer follow-up and prospect follow-up. And we haven't even talked yet about prospect follow-up.

Back to the customer. Guerrillas send their customers another note within 90 days, this time informing them of a new and related product or service. Possibly it's a new offering that the Guerrilla Mortgage Broker now provides. And maybe it's a product or service offered by one of the Guerrilla's fusion marketing partners.

Guerrillas are very big on forging marketing alliances with businesses throughout the community — and using the Internet, throughout the Country. These tie-ins enable them to increase their marketing exposure while reducing their marketing costs, a noble goal.

After six months, the customer hears from the Guerrilla again, this time with the preview announcement of an upcoming event. Nine months after the closing, the Guerrilla sends a note asking the customer for the names of three people who might benefit from being included on the Guerrilla's mailing list. A simple form and postpaid envelope is provided. Because the Guerrilla has been keeping in touch with the customer — and because only three names are requested — the customer often supplies the names.

After one year, the customer receives an anniversary card celebrating the one-year anniversary of the closing. Perhaps a coupon for a discount is snuggled in the envelope.

Fifteen months after the closing, the customer receives a questionnaire, filled with questions designed to give the Guerrilla insights into the customer. The questionnaire has a paragraph at the start that says, "We know your time is valuable, but the reason we're asking so many questions is because the more we know about you, the better service we can be to you." This makes sense. The customer completes and mails the questionnaire.

Perhaps after 18 months, the customer receives an announcement of still more new products and services that tie in with the original purchase. And the beat goes on. The customer, rather than being a one-time buyer, becomes a repeat buyer, becomes the kind of person who refers others to the Guerrilla's business. A bond is formed. The bond intensifies with time and follow-up.

Let me put this on numeric terms to burn it into your mind. Suppose you are not a Guerrilla and do not understand follow-up. Let's say you earn a $2,000 profit every time you make a sale. Okay, a customer walks in, fills out an application, gets qualified, closes the loan, and leaves (simplified, I know). You pocket $2,000 in profits and that one customer was worth $2,000 to you. Hey, $2,000 isn't all bad. But let's say you were a Guerrilla.

That means you send the customer the thank-you note, the one-month note, the three-month note, the six-month note, the nine-month note, the anniversary card, the questionnaire, the constant alerting of new offerings. The customer, instead of closing one loan during the course of a year, closes two loans. That same customer refers your business to five other people. Your bond is not merely for the length of the transaction but for as long as say, 20 years.

Because of your follow-up, that one customer is worth $4,000,000 to you. So that's your choice: $2,000 with no follow-up or $4,000,000 with follow-up. And the cost of follow-up is not high because you already have the name of the person.

The cost of prospect follow-up is also not high and for the same reason as with customers. Prospect follow-up is different from customer follow-up. For one thing, you can't send a thank-you note — yet. But you can consistently follow up, never giving up and realizing that if you're second in line, you'll get the business when the business that's first in line messes up — and they will foul up. You know how? Of course you do. They'll fail to follow up enough.

GUERRILLA EXERCISE:

1. Make a list of three ways you can enlarge the size of each transaction.

    a. _____

    b. _____

    c. _____

2. Make a list of five ways you can follow up with each customer.

    a. _____

    b. _____

    c. _____

3. Make a list of three ways you can follow up with each prospect.

    a. _____

    b. _____

    c. _____

GUERRILLA ACTION STEPS:

A. Keep track for one month of the follow-up mail, postcards, telephone contacts and email follow ups that you receive from businesses that you patronize. Ask yourself which follow-ups motivate a purchase on your part.

B. Think back about the purchases that you've made during the past year. Determine which ones were the result of the business enlarging the size of the transaction. Then, figure which of those methods that you might utilize.

DAVID L. HANCOCK

Guerrilla Marketing
In Tough Times: Part V

Mining Your Customer List For Fun And Profit

Your best source of new customers during tough times is your list of old customers. It's as though you live next to a bountiful gold mine, owned entirely by you — but you never take a single nugget, and you consistently complain about your lack of profits.

A sad scene, yet one that is repeated daily in every State of the Union. This shouldn't happen to you — but the chances are that it does, and this section is devoted to stopping it.

The bountiful gold mine is your customer list. On that roster of wonderful people are the names of customers who know other wonderful people, poised and ready to get onto your customer list themselves. All they need is a gentle nudge. And who do you think is the chief nudger?

You are — if you're a Guerrilla. If you're canny enough to know that the richest source of new customers is old customers, then you're ready to mine that list for names that will be forthcoming — and on a yearly basis at that — if you simply ask for them. Is it that easy? You bet.

The man who lead the nation in insurance policy sales a few years ago was interviewed, focusing upon his astounding success — because he sold twice as many policies as the agent who finished in second place.

He explained that as soon as his client would sign on the dotted line, this agent would reach into his attaché case and withdraw a large memo pad. In the presence of his new client, he would write numbers on a blank page: 1, 2, 3, 4 and 5. Then, he'd ask his client for the names of five people who might benefit from a policy such as the client just purchased. The client, feeling positive, almost always furnished the names. Five isn't an unreasonably high number, plus it's nice and specific.

Guerrillas learn a lesson from this example. So they put into writing a Guerrilla referral program. How do you get such a program to work? Four steps:

1. At the time of the initial closing, ask for the names of five people who might benefit from the product or service your customer just closed.

2. In six months, send a brief letter reminding them that you know the importance of customers, then asking for the names of three people who could benefit by doing business with you. Provide a postpaid return envelope.

3. A year after that, ask for the names of four people who could gain by becoming your customers. Perhaps this time you'll send a little gift, whether or not the customer furnishes names.

4. Once a year, for as long as you're in business, ask your customers for the names of three, four or five people who might gain by becoming your customers. Because of your Guerrilla follow-up, expect a healthy response.

When it's appropriate, ask if you can use the name of the customer when contacting the prospect he or she recommended. Talk about door-openers! Thank the customer for taking the time to provide these valuable names. This Guerrilla referral program is simply common sense, yet how can you explain the absence of such programs at most Mortgage Broker Shops? Think there might be a connection between high business failure rates and few referral programs?

Guerrillas know that it costs six times more to make a sale to a prospect than to an existing customer, so they do everything in their power to increase the size of their customer list, then market with Guerrilla gusto to customers and acquaintances of customers. Just realize that along with the repeat business of customers can become a gold mine of names of future customers. Be sure you stake a claim to your fair share of nuggets.

The cost of an active referral program is tiny compared to the potential for profits such a program can mean. The best way to get the names of new customers from old customers? Simply ask for them.

As a Guerrilla, you've been staying in touch, so your customers want you to succeed and will happily comply with your request for say, three names. Ask for them, provide a postpaid envelope, and you'll soon see this tactic is pure gold. There are other ways to tap into your enormous referral power:

Identify potential references. List everyone with whom you have worked in the past three years, and others who know you well.

1. Note on your list what you would like a reference to do. There is more than one kind of reference: use of their name, calls for you, and written testimonials. Be specific. Think especially of what you would like past customers to say. You'll be surprised at how willing they are to say it.

2. Ask pleasantly. Asking politely generates good references. Everybody understands the need for a business reference. It's a reasonable thing to ask for. If properly asked, most people will applaud good work.

3. Request name use. First, phone and ask the potential references if you can use their names — either in talking with a potential customer or on your company brochure. Allow them the chance to say no.

4. Get telephone references. You can tell by people's voice tones if their references will be good. If references agree to your using their names, ask if they will take phone inquiries. Create a stable of references who will speak highly of you when called.

5. Obtain a letter. If the telephone reference is better than average, ask for it in writing. Tell the reference that a few short words will do, such as, "Ms. Atwood's service was outstanding. We intend to use her on 100% of our future transactions."

Why don't people give more referrals? Because they're afraid you'll foul up and they'll be blamed. Guerrillas continue to develop new customers all the time because know they're losing old customers all the time. Here's how:

1% of customers die.

3% move away.

5% develop other business relationships.

9% leave for competitive reasons.

14% are dissatisfied with the product or service.

68% leave due to an indifference on the part of an employee.

The way around these irrevocable statistics? With a referral program that is active, alive, constantly used and part of the way you run your business.

GUERRILLA EXERCISE:

1. Look at your customer list and realize deep in your heart that it's your most precious business asset. Used properly, it can lead to untold profits... and with a minimal investment on your part.

2. Create a referral program in writing. It should call for you to contact these customers on a regular basis — not merely for follow-up marketing, but with the purpose of getting names of potential future customers. This is especially easy with email.

GUERRILLA ACTION STEPS:

A. Actually write the letter you will send to customers, the letter that asks for the names of people who might benefit from doing business with you.

B. Select five customers you will call by phone to secure the names of people who are potential customers. Call them and tell them that you'd appreciate these names as a way of holding down your marketing costs. By seeing how simple it is to get names, you'll be motivated to call more customers -- or ask one of your employees to do it for you. Hint: It helps the most if you are the one who makes the call.

DAVID L. HANCOCK

Guerrilla Marketing
In Tough Times: Part VI

Community Involvement In Tough Times

G uerrillas know well that people want to do business with friends instead of strangers if at all possible. You must have their insight that you dive into an ocean of friends with community involvement. You become involved with the community by helping it. It becomes involved with you by helping you. Marketers need friends. From these friends come business associates, marketing partners, investors, employees, customers, prospects, suppliers and referrals.

Becoming involved with the community means more than joining clubs. It means contributing your brains and energy to the community. It means working hard to make your community a better place. You get to prove your conscientiousness and noble efforts with the work you do instead of the words you say.

One of the keys to marketing — keeping it very personal, because the more personal the marketing the better — is in establishing relationships through networking. And one of the richest sources of networking opportunities is the community. You serve on committees. You go to little league games. You help set up parades, holiday decorating programs, Thanksgiving Day turkey races, Fourth of July celebrations. People see you in action. They see that you're a person of action, a person who keeps their word. So when you say something in a marketing context, they tend to believe you. When you make an offer, they know it's not going to be bogus. You've proved yourself in the community.

There are wrong ways to demonstrate community involvement as well. If you volunteer to work on a committee but are never available for meetings, or if you sponsor a little league team and don't show up for games, you're proving yourself to be crass and superficial, probably sucking up the community to get business instead of working for it for altruistic reasons. Consumers are more sophisticated than ever these days. People know the difference between serving the community and serving yourself. If you're not willing to devote honest time and energy to your community, you're better off skipping this weapon and leaving it to the real Guerrillas in your community. I just hope for your sake that none are your direct competitors.

Your community is not merely defined by geography. Guerrillas become involved with their industrial community, though it may reach from coast to coast, or across the ocean. Digital communities are springing up all over the place as the world goes online. Whatever the size or scope of your community, the Guerrilla rule remains the same: do unto others as they hope you will do unto them. As part of the community, they are hoping for your help, not your hype.

While you're involved with your community, be sure that you're attuned to their problems. Listen for the ouch. Guerrillas know that it's easier to sell the solution to a problem than to sell a positive benefit. That's why they position themselves as problem-solvers.

A well-known axiom of marketing has always been that it is much simpler to sell the solution to a problem than it is to sell a positive benefit. For this reason, Guerrillas position their shops to be ace problem-solvers... especially during tough times.

They hone in on the problems confronting their prospects, and then offer their products or services as solutions to the problems. Almost all individuals and companies are beset with problems of one sort or another. Your job, as a right-thinking Guerrilla, is to spot those problems. One of the ways to do this is through networking in your community.

Networking is not a time to toot your own trombone, but to ask questions, to listen carefully to the answers, and to keep your marketing radar attuned to the presence of problems. After learning what the problems are, you can then contact the prospect and talk about their problems and the solutions you have to those nasty dilemmas.

You can also learn of problems that require solving at trade shows, professional association meetings, prospect questionnaires, and even sales calls.

As you already know, people do not buy shampoo; they buy clean, great-looking hair. That means selling a benefit. A way that some shampoos have achieved profits is by reassuring people that the shampoo cleans hair, then stressing that it solves the problem of unmanageable hair — a benefit and a solution to a problem.

Right now, products and services that are enjoying success are those that help people quit smoking, lose weight, earn more money, improve health, grow hair, eliminate wrinkles, and save time. These are problem-solving products and services.

You can be sure that some of these can also be positioned as offerings that accentuate a positive, but savvy company presidents saw to it that their offerings were positioned as things that could eliminate a negative. Your biggest job is to be sure your products and services do the same.

Perhaps you'll have to undergo a major repositioning. That's not bad if it improves your profits. Far more doors will be open to you if you can achieve it.

Maybe you know right off, the major problems your prospects face. Your marketing should highlight these problems. Then, it should offer your product or service as the ideal solution. If you don't know the problems, then knock yourself out learning them. Regardless of the benefits you offer, realize that their importance is generally overshadowed by the problems confronting a prospect.

It's really not that difficult to position your offering as a problem-solver. But once you do, you'll find that the task of marketing and selling become a whole lot easier in a hurry. You'll have to examine your offerings in the light of how they affect your prospects. So what if they are state-of-the-art? That pales in comparison with their ability to reduce your prospect's overhead. So what if they are lower in price than they used to be? That's nothing compared with their ability to help your prospects combat loneliness.

Those prospects care about saving money, to be sure. But they care far more about feeling alone and unloved. If you can solve that problem for your prospects, buying what you sell will be very easy for them.

Prospects don't really care about your company; they care about their problems. If you can solve them, then prospects will care a great deal about your company, and they'll want to buy what you are selling.

Guerrillas lean upon case histories to prove their problem-solving acumen. They make certain to include in their marketing plan both the problem and the solution — to guide those who create marketing materials from wandering off in the wrong direction.

Sales training in Guerrilla Mortgage shops involves a discussion of problems, problem-spotting, problem discussing, and problem-solving. Loan Officers learn the nature of prospect problems from one another. Sharing their insights helps the entire company.

Amazingly, even though this all makes sense, many mortgage companies are unaware of the importance of problem-solving. They're so wrapped up in the glories of their product or service that they are oblivious to how well it solves problems. So they sell features and neglect benefits. They sell the obtaining of positives instead of the eliminating of negatives.

Keep the concept of problem-solving alive in your mind, your marketing materials, your sales presentations, and your company mission. Be sure your employees are tuned into the same wave length. Once this happens, I have a feeling that you're going to be one happy Guerrilla.

GUERRILLA EXERCISE:

1. Make a list of the community organizations where you live — or online communities where you can become involved. Then, list the things you can do for the community. Don't offer to do anything that you can't accomplish with excellence. So be selective.

2. Make a phone call, send a letter, or send an email volunteering your services. Take the time to actually do it after you've completed this section. He who hesitates is not a Guerrilla.

GUERRILLA ACTION STEPS:

A. Make a list of the problems that your business can solve. The longer your list, the more profits you'll earn during an economic downturn.

B. Examine all of your marketing efforts, online and offline; to be sure you address your problem-solving skills. Make the necessary changes to ensure that you're putting those skills in front of your audience. Don't neglect the positive benefits you offer, but highlight your ability to solve problems.

DAVID L. HANCOCK

Guerrilla Marketing
In Tough Times: Part VII

Attracting New Business In Tough Times

When the going gets tough, the tough get new business. Many of your competitors have pulled in their horns and cut back on their marketing. This means new opportunities for you to get new customers. The obtaining of precious new business is a whole lot easier than you may have imagined — but only if you have the mindset of the Guerrilla.

One of the least understood secrets of successful marketing is the ease with which new business may be won. As powerful as you may be with that knowledge, your power increases when you comprehend the importance of gaining that new business in the first place.

You already know that it costs you six times more to sell something to a new customer than to an existing customer — which is why Guerrillas market so caringly and consistently to their customers — there is a constant need to increase your customer base. Therefore, you're got to be willing to turn cartwheels in order to get a human being converted into a real live paying customer. Break even or even lose money in the quest for a new customer because your investment in securing these precious souls will be returned many-fold.

Once your prospects become customers, they're a source of profits for life — because Guerrillas like you know the crucial importance of non-stop follow-up. The follow-up increases your profits while decreasing your cost or marketing.

But let's get back to those non-customers and consider a potent Guerrilla tactic to win their business and transfer them from the twilight zone to your customer list, where they belong. The tactic begins with a phrase. A powerful Guerrilla phrase to emblazon amidst your memory cells is "pilot project."

It is often difficult to get a company or a person to agree to do business with you, especially in a shaky economy. It is much simpler to get them to agree to a mere pilot project. Even if companies or individuals are unhappy with their current providers, they may be reluctant to sever the relationship and sign up with you — just in case you turn out to be flaky.

But you defuse that reluctance when you assure them that you don't want to get married — and get all their business. You only want to become engaged — and get a simple pilot project. That's certainly not asking for much.

Pilot projects are very tempting to companies and to individuals because they allow these good people to see if you're as good as you say you are, without going too far out on a limb. Even if the project is a bust, it was only a pilot project. No big deal.

But if the project is a success — well then, that certainly indicates that a larger project should be undertaken, then a larger one still, and eventually, all the business. Moral? It's tough to get an okay for all the new business. But it is far less tough to get an okay for a pilot project.

The concept of aiming for pilot projects may be applied as easily to a service business as a product business. If you perform services, offer to perform them for only part of the customer's needs, not all of them. Offer to perform them for a test period only, something like six weeks or so — maybe even less if you feel that less time will be enough for you to prove your worth and value.

If you sell services, request that during the pilot project, you be given prominent display, proper signage, and ample exposure. But because it's only a pilot project, ask for this only for a limited time, or with a limited number of applications. Will your products generate profits? This simple pilot project will tell.

Guerrillas are wary of wooing new business by offering discounts — because they know darned well that customers who purchase by price alone are the worst possible kind, disloyal, expensive to maintain, and in the end, only one-ninth as profitable as loyal customers who stick around because of value or service, quality or selection. But these self-same Guerrillas are very willing even to lose money on customers — for the first sale only — if the customers focus on things other than mere cost.

Pilot projects are rarely profit producers all by themselves. But they open the door to a world where profits abound, a world where relationships are lasting. That's why savvy companies and individuals say "yes" to offers of pilot projects. These projects are inexpensive learning and high potential earning opportunities. Hey! Why not do a pilot project on pilot projects?

I am very aware that during a spiraling economy, you've got to make a dynamite proposal — even to get the go sign for a pilot project. I'm also aware that many businesses fall on their faces when they make a proposal. Having secured an appointment to make a proposal, Guerrillas stand out and shine.

They know that it's at proposal time that the rubber meets the road. To get the best ride Possible, you've got to present a Guerrilla proposal. This section will show you how to create one.

There are poor proposals, which rarely get the business for you. There are good proposals, which might get the business for you. And then, there are Guerrilla proposals, which usually get the business for you. If you present anything but a Guerrilla proposal, it means that all the marketing you've done up till that time has probably been wasted. Sheer agony.

The companies that get the business realize that all the time and energy they've put into wooing a prospective customer has been mere groundwork for the dazzling display of business shrewdness that will be made apparent when they get down to the business of making an actual proposal.

Guerrillas follow these 10 steps to make sure that their courtship activities lead to a long-term business marriage — destined to flourish and prosper.

1. Guerrillas are always positive that they have qualified their prospects so that the marriage doesn't die during the honeymoon. Getting your prospect's attention is only a tiny part of assuring a lasting relationship. When your prospect shakes hands with you and says "Let's do it!" — You've got to be certain that both of you will gain. You must be right for them and they must be right for you. Chemistry counts in both people-to-people marriages and in business-to-business pairings.

2. Guerrillas start immediately to warm up the relationship by building rapport with their prospects. They never want to walk into a prospect's office or conference room as a complete stranger. That's why they see their job as forging a bond before making the proposal. They know well that it's much easier to do business with friends than strangers.

3. Guerrillas identify a real need that their prospects have and know in their hearts that they can fill that need better than anyone else. They keep foremost in their minds the truism that people give their

business to firms that can help them solve their problems and exploit their opportunities.

4. Guerrillas make absolutely certain that the prospect to whom they are making their proposal can use their products or services right now, and not at some future date down the road. They present their proposals only to people who are the ultimate decision-makers and can give them the go-ahead immediately without having to check with higher authorities. During an economic slowdown, this is of paramount importance.

5. Guerrillas rehearse their presentation till they've got it down pat. They decide ahead of time exactly what they want to show and tell, then plan intelligently, back their chosen words with graphics, and always ask for the order at the conclusion of the proposal. Non-Guerrillas may make a decent proposal, but usually fail to ask outright for what they want

6. Guerrillas prepare a document to leave with their prospects right after the proposal has been presented. The document summarizes the high points of the proposal, is completely self-contained, and includes important facts and figures that might have bogged down the actual presentation.

7. Guerrillas design their proposals in a way that addresses their prospect's goals clearly and unmistakably. They are able to do this with a single sentence that proves they are directed and oriented to those goals. They find ways to repeat that sentence several times during the presentation of their proposal — up front, in the middle, at the end, and in the written document they give to their prospect when the presentation is completed.

8. Guerrillas present their proposals in a logical manner so that one point flows naturally to the next, making

the proposal very simple to follow. They know that the organization of their proposal is nearly as important as the content. Their proposals prove beyond doubt that they are qualified to get the business, and then that they are particularly qualified and deserving of the business right now.

9. Guerrillas speak and write in the first person, aligning everything they say with the prospect's business. They make it a point to talk about the prospect's business and not about their own. In fact, they only speak of their own business in terms of how it can help the prospect's business. This requires homework and Guerrillas always do their homework before presenting any proposal.

10. Guerrillas are quick to use the services of a talented art director or a power-point presentation to help them reinforce their points visually, knowing that points made to the eye are 68% more effective than the same points made to the ear. They always try to visualize what they are saying, and they realize that if the visuals are shoddy or look home-made, they are sabotaging themselves.

When you are making a proposal, you must make the prospect like you, like your company, and love what your company can do for them. You must then actually ask for the business at the conclusion of the presentation. Never underestimate the brute power of straightforwardness.

Because Guerrillas are ultra-keen about follow-up, they follow-up their proposals with a thank-you note within 24 hours of the presentation. That follow-up also includes a phone call to be sure no questions are left unanswered, to see if there is anything else the prospect would like to know, and to establish a start date for doing business together. The follow-up should be directed to the person who has the authority to say "yes."

The more data you have about your prospect, the better your proposal will be and the more likely it is to land the business for you. The better you prove that you understand the prospect's competitive situation, the more likely that prospect will want your help. And the better the chemistry is between your people and the prospect's people, the more likely it is that you'll get exactly what you want.

Never fail to keep in mind the power of a personal bond. And never forget that when you're making a proposal, your three greatest allies are your knowledge of the prospect, your enthusiasm during the presentation, and the personal bonding you have already established.

GUERRILLA EXERCISE:

1. Make a list of prospects who have not yet been converted to customers. Then, select the 10 who will most likely be most profitable for your business. Pull out all the stops when contacting these 10 and learn what works for you and what doesn't. After you've completed your high-potency marketing to those 10, take on the rest of your prospect list, using what you learned during the original 10.

2. Create a proposal for the single best prospect of all. Then knock yourself out making an appointment to make the proposal. You may earn the business and you'll definitely learn more about your ability to create winning proposals.

GUERRILLA ACTION STEPS:

A. Put into writing the specifics of a pilot project you can perform for a client. The more specifics you have, the easier it will be to sell that project.

B. Practice making your proposal to a current customer. Ask that customer for feedback and suggestions. This will not only deepen your relationship with that customer, but will also help you hone your presenting skills and the quality of your proposal.

DAVID L. HANCOCK

Guerrilla Marketing
In Tough Times: Part VIII

The Importance Of Service During Tough Times

I f ever there was a time to emphasize your impeccable service, it's when the economy is heading South. Sure, all business owners care about their customers, but Guerrilla marketers prove they care.

It's very easy to care about your customers, even easier to say that you care. But unless you take steps to show them that you care, they might be wooed away by a competitor. Your marketing can say all the right words and tell customers how important they are to you. But you've got to prove your dedication to customers — and prospects — by taking concrete steps beyond mere words.

Guerrillas know that there's a world of difference between customer care and customer attention. Many companies lavish attention upon their customers, but only the Guerrillas excel at caring and know how to make customers feel sincerely cared for. Here are 20 ways they do it:

1. Prepare a written document outlining the principles of your customer service. This should come from the president, but everyone should know what it says and be ready to live up to it.

2. Establish support systems that give clear instructions for gaining and maintaining service superiority. They help you out service any competitor by giving more to customers and solving problems before they arise.

3. Develop a precise measurement of superb customer service and reward employees who practice it consistently. Many will if you hire people who really want to render great service and don't just do it because they should.

4. Be certain that your passion for customer service runs rampant throughout your company and not just at the top. Everyone should feel it.

5. Do all that you must to instill in employees who meet your customers a truly deep appreciation of the value of customer service. They should see how this service relates to your profits and to their future.

6. Be genuinely committed to providing more customer service excellence than anyone else. This commitment must be so powerful that every one of your customers can sense it.

7. Be sure that everyone in your company who deals with customers pays very close attention to the customer. Each customer should feel unique and special after they've contacted you or been contacted by you.

8. Ask questions of your customers, and then listen carefully to their answers. Ask customers to expand upon their answers.

9. Stay in touch with your customers. Do it with letters, email, postcards, newsletters, phone calls, questionnaires and, if you can, at trade shows.

10. Nurture a human bond as well as a business bond with customers and prospects. Do favors for them. Educate them. Help them. Give gifts. Play favorites. Take them out to the ballgame or the opera. Your customers deserve to be treated this special.

11. Recognize that your customers have needs and expectations. You've got to meet their needs and exceed their expectations. Always? Always.

12. Understand why successful corporations such as 3M define service as "conformance to customer requirements." This means that true Guerrilla service is just what the customer wants it to be. Not easy, but necessary.

13. Keep alert for trends, and then respond to them. McDonald's operates under the axiom, "We lead the industry by following our customers."

14. Share information with people on the front line. Disney workers meet regularly to talk about improving their service. Information-sharing is easier than ever with new communications technologies. Share information with customers and prospects by having a website that is loaded with helpful data. More and more, this is becoming mandatory.

15. Because customers are humans, observe birthdays and anniversaries. Constant communication should be your goal. If you find an article in the media that will help a customer, send a copy of the article to that customer. Have you ever received such an article from one of your service provider? Probably not. That's why your attention to a customer will stand out so brightly.

16. Consider holding "mixers" so customers can get to know your people better and vice-versa. Mixers are breeding grounds for human bonds.

17. Invest in phone equipment that makes your business sound friendly, easy to do business with, easy to contact and quick to respond. Again, technology makes this easier than ever. Along with phone equipment, let customers know they can contact you by fax and email.

18. Design your physical layout for efficiency, clarity of signage, lighting, handicap accessibility and simplicity. Everything should be easy to find.

19. Act on the knowledge that what customers value most are attention, dependability, promptness and competence. They just love being treated as individuals and being referred to by their name. Don't you?

20. When it comes to customer service, Nordstrom is a superstar, though Disney gives them a run for their money, and so do the Ritz-Carlton Hotels. The Nordstrom service manual is eloquent in its simplicity: "Use your good judgment in all situations. There will be no additional rules."

Guerrillas send postage-paid questionnaire cards and letters asking for suggestions. They fix the trouble areas revealed and know well the relationship between proving their care and success.

GUERRILLA EXERCISE:

1. Put into writing a list of the ways you offer remarkable good service. The longer your list, the easier it will be for you to thrive during a rugged economy. Augment that list by adding three items of service that you have not stressed before. When all else is equal, the company that offers the best and the most services is the one that will win the customer. Now, post that list on your website.

2. List the technologies you now employ to render superlative service: a fax machine, voice-mail, an auto-responder, a toll-free number, a cell phone, a pager — so that you make customer contact as simple as possible. To learn of a new service that makes it simpler than ever, visit www.500PLUS.com. They let you have a toll-free 500 number along with a matching website and email address. The cost is far less than you'd imagine. Most of all be sure you have a content-rich website that sees things from the customer's point of view.

GUERRILLA ACTION STEPS:

A. Think back upon services rendered by other companies, services that impressed you. Try to adapt those services to your own company so that you are a stand-out when it comes to service. Nordstrom, Disney and Ritz-Carlton Hotels conduct special meetings that address nothing but service. Employee and customer suggestions are solicited. Do the same for your company. With a limited budget and a tight economy, exceptional service can make the crucial difference.

B. Think of one service that is offered by none of your competitors, a service that your customers are sure to appreciate. Then, do all in your power to market this service. By doing so, you'll be able to jump start your reputation for great service.

Guerrilla Marketing
In Tough Times: Part IX

Making Yourself The Talk Of The Town

Word-of-mouth marketing referrals come to companies automatically if they utilize a broad array of marketing weapons over a long period of time. But Guerrillas, as patient as they are, try to shortcut the process of obtaining positive word-of-mouth.

One way they do it is with brochures printed especially for people who are first-time buyers. This is because of a phenomenon called the "moment of maximum satisfaction." That moment lasts from the moment a person closes a loan till 30 days past that time. During this period the person is most likely to spread the word about his transaction, conveying his enthusiasm and yours to all who will listen. If you hand such a person your new customer brochure, you are putting the right words in the right mouths at the right time.

Small wonder your word-of-mouth will pick up.

Another way to obtain healthy word-of-mouth marketing is to ask this question: Who else do your customers patronize? Then, do a favor for those people. Here's an example: A restaurant opened in my community and asked that question. The answer turned out to be: hairstylists. So the restaurant distributed coupons good for two free dinners to all the styling salon owners within a two-mile radius of the restaurant. The salon owners would eat their free meals, then talk up the restaurant in their salons, generating loads of business for the restaurant. By recognizing that the salon was the nerve-center of the community, the restaurant was able to succeed without spending one cent for advertising.

You can also become the talk of the town with public relations. Public relations means exactly what it says. But it is also accurate to say that it means publicity-free stories and news about you and/or your company in newspapers, magazines, and newsletters, on radio and TV, and in any other type of media.

Here's what is good about publicity: It is free. It is very believable. It gives you and your company a lot of credibility and stature. It helps establish the identity of your business. It gives you authority. It is read by a large number of people. It is remembered.

Many entrepreneurs feel that there is no such thing as bad publicity; that as long as you get your name out there before the public, that's a fine thing. But Guerrillas know that bad publicity leads to bad word-of-mouth marketing, known to spread faster than wildfire. Bad publicity is bad. Good publicity is great.

There are even some bad things about good publicity, though I only mean bad in a relative sense. You have no control over publicity. You have no say-so as to when it runs. You have no control over how it is presented. It is rarely repeated. You cannot buy it. You cannot ensure its accuracy.

On balance, however, publicity is an excellent weapon in any well-stocked marketing arsenal. And any marketing plan that fails to include some effort at public relations is a marketing plan that isn't going all out. And during the days of a faltering economy, it's a marketing plan bordering on stupidity.

Public relations offers, as an unstated but ultra-valuable benefit, decades of staying power. Reprints of positive publicity can be framed, made parts of brochures, included in ads, put onto flipcharts, and leaned upon for precious credibility. The day the story appears is a heartwarming one, but the years afterward are when the marketing power abounds. When you can do it, use reprints of the story to empower your marketing. But you can't always do it.

When Jay Conrad Levinson was advertising his self-published book *Earning Money Without a Job* (since revised for the 90s and published in 1991 by Henry Holt and Company, New York) in various magazines and national newspapers, he was spending about $1000 per ad. Each ad was bringing in about $3000 in sales. The book was not available in bookstores and could be purchased only through my mail-order ad. Then a reporter from the San Francisco Chronicle purchased a copy of my book. Because Jay lived in the vicinity, and because the reporter took a liking to the book, he called to see if he could go to Jay's home and interview Jay, and asked if he could bring along a photographer. It didn't take Jay long to extend a warm welcome to him and his camera-bearing associate.

The interview lasted about an-hour and included a brief photo session. A few days later, an article about Jay and his book appeared in the main news section of the newspaper. Accompanying it was a photo of Jay. Well into the article was the address to which the $10 purchase price (now it's less) could be sent. Within a week, Jay received more than $10,000 worth of orders! The article had not solicited orders, did not really try to sell the book, and mentioned the address and selling price in a place where only serious readers of the article would find them. More than $10,000 in sales, and the marketing didn't cost Jay one penny.

As wonderful as Jay felt about the results, he felt just as frustrated at not being able to repeat the process. Jay sent the article to other newspapers, letting them know he was available for interviews. He continued to advertise the book, still achieving a fair degree of success. But never again has he been able to earn so much money with so little effort. Because his mama didn't raise a moron, he made reprints of the article and used them as parts of mailings and press kits. So he did receive a bit more mileage from the publicity. Although he knew of similar stories, and indeed had arranged and taken part in them, never has the value of PR hit home as sweetly as in that instance.

The reporter felt that his book was newsy, since it promised honest information on how people could earn a good living without having to hold down a job. And that is probably the single most important factor in obtaining free publicity: providing news worth publicizing.

A fascinating P.S. to that PR tale is what happened to the reporter, Mel Ziegler, who interviewed Jay. He took the concepts of the book to heart, quit his job at the Chronicle, and opened a store, the first of an empire, called Banana Republic.

Before you read one more word, read these: the media need you more than you need them. They need news. They hunger for news. Their unquenchable need for news is why people read them, listen to them and view them. If you have news or can make news or can create news, you are exactly what the media is looking for.

Marcia Yudkin, who knows a thing or six about publicity, gives us six steps to free publicity, based upon her book by the same name. I alert you to them here:

1. Find a news angle for your headline.

2. Present the basic facts for the angle of your headline in the first paragraph of your press release.

3. Gather or create a lively, fascinating quote that elaborates on the basic facts for the second paragraph of your release.

4. Elaborate still further on the basic facts in your third paragraph.

5. End your release with the nitty-gritty details about prices, addresses, dates, phone numbers, and registration data if any. Keep this to one paragraph.

6. Email it, send it out, or hand it to your buddies who work for the media. It helps immensely if you have a specific editor or produce who you can refer to by name.

How do you generate something newsy for the news media? Announce something new about your business or group. Write about what's unique and unusual about your business. Tell of an upcoming event. Write of the connection between your offering and what's in the news right now. Announce the results of a survey or research poll you conducted or even one you read about. Tell the community who won your sales contest. Tie in with a holiday or anniversary, especially a city event. Write of the connection between your business and a current trend. Make a controversial claim or at least, a very surprising claim. Make a humorous announcement. Put it into an eye-catching headline and you're off to the races for free publicity, appearances on talk shows, and profits for a minimal investment.

Let me clarify here that if you want to, you can pay for public relations. You can hire a PR person, pay him or her a monthly or project fee — anywhere from $500 to $25,000 per month — and let that person do what is necessary to secure free publicity. PR people are experts at it. They have the contacts, the experience, and the insights. They have made all the errors, they have learned from them, and they are usually well worth their fees. But because you are a Guerrilla, I want to let you know in this chapter of ways you can do what PR people do. That way, you'll be able to get the publicity and you won't have to pay anyone a dime.

Moment of truth time: The best way to succeed at public relations is to have publicity contacts — people at the media who you know on a first — name basis. It's one thing to mail a proper press kit to the proper managing editor at a publication. It's another thing to call Nancy at the paper and say, "Nancy, let's have lunch tomorrow. I have some information that will definitely interest your readers and I want you to have it first. I'll pop for the lunch."

Nancy, because she enjoys free lunches, but primarily because she knows and trusts you, has lunch with you. Never forget how hungry the news media are for news. If you have real news, they'll listen. So Nancy listens and the next day, there's a story about your product or service or company in her newspaper. When you pay a PR pro a steep fee, you're paying for a gob of Nancys, and those publicity contacts are usually well worth the price.

One of the most important public relations tools is the annual report. As a rule, entrepreneurs don't publish one. But why not? It need not conform to the usual annual report sent to shareholders. It need not talk money. It can be a report that contains information valuable to your customers. When you do publish such an annual report, send some copies to the media. Let them enjoy your creativity. Nudge them to give that creativity some "ink." And by all means, send your annual report to your prospects.

Members of the press are frequently invited to "press parties." At these parties, cocktails or beverages and a meal or hors d'oeuvres are served, and frequently a presentation is made. It's a short one, but affective and hard-selling. The purpose is to woo the press with wining and dining, then win their hearts with a dramatic presentation of the facts. Naturally, the facts are about a new business or a new direction for an old business. It's no surprise that the press coverage following these parties is tremendous. Guerrillas hold their press parties at unique places such as ferryboats, railroad cars traveling to interesting destinations, penthouses, haunted houses, parks, baseball diamonds, and art galleries.

A major-league PR pro once told me that nearly 80 percent of the news is "planted" — sent to the media by publicity firms and lobbying groups. Sometimes planted news deals with political topics; sometimes it deals with industrial topics; and sometimes it deals with products or people. That PR pro repeated what insiders know-newspapers are hungry for real news. If you can furnish it, they'll gladly publish it. But telling a newspaper that you are having a sale is not news. Informing a radio station that you have started a business is not news. News needs a slant to it, a hook that will grab them.

Guerrillas love the free press coverage they get from the big newspapers, but they rarely overlook the small ones. There are many of them and nearly all of them count. They never send more than one release at a time, and they are quick to learn of the myriad of PR opportunities online, discussed in *Guerrilla Marketing Online, Second Edition,* by Jay Conrad Levinson.

The best marketing plans usually call for a combination of advertising and public relations. The two go hand in hand. One is highly credible but gives you no control. The other has less credibility but gives you complete control. Together, they supply most of the pieces of the marketing puzzle.

When the circus comes to town and you put up a sign, that's advertising. If you put that sign on the back of the elephant and you market the elephant through town, that's sales promotion. If the elephant, with the sign still on his back, tramples through the mayor's flower garden and the paper reports it, that's publicity. If you can get the mayor to laugh about it and forgive the elephant and then ride in the circus with no hard feelings, then you truly understand Guerrilla publicity.

Advertising is the most expensive method of getting out the word. Direct marketing is the next most expensive method.

Being online comes in next when it comes to expense. And PR is the least expensive, but is the most time-consuming.

If you know PR, you should know what the media does not like. It's a pretty obvious list: hemming and hawing, wasted time, frivolous questions, incomplete sentences, bad writing, people who cannot take no for a an answer, people who don't really believe in what they're calling or writing about, ugly persistence, demanding natures, bad listeners, people who constantly interrupt, lack of common sense, and blatant attempts to advertise under the guide of real news.

Why does well-intention PR go awry? Same reason businesses fail. Same reason marketing fails. Same reason advertising fails. It's failure to follow-up. If you're too busy to make an average of four phone calls for every media outlet you've contacted, you should turn your PR over to a pro who has the time and expertise you may lack.

If you have a mortgage shop and send out a release that says, "Best rate in town," you're likely to be greeted by a big ho-hum. But if you sponsor a charity drive, put up a display and sign in front of your office, link up with a local celebrity, and the invite the media to check you out for a story, they now have a newsy and valid reason to do a story about your mortgage shop. Did I say it was easy? Never did. Did I say it helps your business? I certainly say that now.

I haven't even mentioned the plethora of public relations and sponsorship opportunities now available on the Internet. Chances abound for you to spread the good word about yourself in cyberspace, as you'll soon discover during your weekly surf. Sponsorship of many sites visited by your prospects is not costly. Just as with offline PR, most online PR is free and requires tireless research on your part. But it will be worth your effort. There are many online sources for building your own media list. Don't rely totally on free resources for your publicity efforts because they typically are not updated frequently enough to be totally accurate or complete. A good way to collect media names which are current and actually writing for your target market is to be alert when reading trade magazines for the writers' names and contact information. Experiment with using personalized news services to receive articles about your industry, then comb those articles for the writers' names.

Just remember what the smartest of the PR pros know all too well: Without publicity, a terrible thing happens: nothing.

GUERRILLA EXERCISE:

1. Make an outline for a "first-time customer" brochure. This is where you'll have the most control over your word-of-mouth marketing.

2. Make a list of other types of businesses that your customers patronize, such as styling salons or a restaurant.

3. Make a list of the media in which you'd most benefit from free publicity. The list should include both online and offline media.

GUERRILLA ACTION STEPS:

A. This is tough, but tough times call for tough tactics. The tactic I recommend most highly for this section is for you to list three people at the media you've selected as most ideal — then get in touch with these people personally. Do it by email, telephone, but best of all — in person. The more media contacts you get, the more you'll become the talk of the town... and at no cost.

B. Come up with a list of three things about your business that are newsy. Perhaps they'll be in the area of product. Possibly they'll connect with your service. Maybe they'll be about new items or services that you offer. The three things you can dream up will be three tickets to free publicity.

DAVID L. HANCOCK

Guerrilla Marketing In Tough Times: Part X

Online Marketing In A Shaky Economy

The newest, biggest, most mysterious, most misunderstood and most promising marketing opportunity in history is the one offered by the advent of the internet. Every day, online marketing gets bigger, better, and more helpful both for marketers and for consumers. Still, three facts must be understood by all who would hope to become online Guerrillas:

1. Online marketing will only work if you understand marketing.

2. Online marketing means a lot more than having a website

3. Online marketing is only one percent of all marketing.

Remember that there are 100 Guerrilla marketing weapons, and online marketing is only one of them. In most cases, you can't market online only with any expectation of success. Yet, the entire media world is becoming fragmented. There are regional editions of magazines, zone editions of newspapers, cable TV stations that reach local communities, local radio stations, targeted mailing lists. Where does everything come together?

It all happens online. Slowly but certainly, people are learning that the whole story exists online — that all the details they must learn before making a purchase are ready to be studied online. The entire Internet phenomenon is part of human progression, and humans learning how to interact in cyberspace is also part of that progression. You don't have to be reminded that progression takes place over a long period of time. The Internet is here and everybody knows it, but not everybody is online yet, and not everybody online is ready to make purchases yet. They will. But not quite yet.

A key fact to remember is that you've got to continue marketing with traditional media. Your website marketing and your website needs marketing. Even when the Internet has achieved a market penetration comparable to that of the telephone, you must continue marketing using time-honored methods. TV revolutionized the marketing scene, but most of the big TV advertisers also market their offerings in places other than the tube. TV is part of their marketing mix, but not the entire mixture.

When marketing with the traditional media, you're going to have to devote time and space to heralding your website because many people will want to know where they can get more information. Your website is where. No media offers you the comprehensiveness of the web. That's why you need it to flesh out your marketing. The world is learning to buy things in a new way and that way is online. But the learning process is still in process.

Pinning down the right way to do Guerrilla marketing online is akin to grabbing a handful of smoke to see what it feels like. Online marketing is the essence of amorphousness and will be for a long time, constantly changing as new heroes of technology try to figure how it can best serve the public while bestowing profits upon the companies employing it. Exciting online technologies are being unveiled so frequently they're becoming humdrum.

Of the billions of dollars being wasted by small business due to a misunderstanding of the comprehensiveness of online marketing and the reality of online consumers — a huge portion is wasted on websites. They are created and posted with obliviousness to their place in the universe.

Guerrillas wouldn't dare waste money on their websites. They know the ground rules in cyberspace when it comes to earning consistent profits on the web. Those profits come when you equally emphasize eight elements.

1. *The first element is planning.* That means you must know ahead of time exactly what you wish to accomplish with your website.

2. *The second element is content.* That's what's going to attract visitors to your site, then keep them coming back for more visits on a regular basis.

3. *The third element is design.* There's a "hang or click" moment when people first see your site. Should they hang around or click away? Design influences their decision.

4. *The fourth element is involvement.* Guerrillas take advantage of the net's interactivity by involving visitors rather than just requiring that they read.

5. *The fifth element is production.* This refers to putting your first four elements online. Easy-to-use software now can do this job for you.

6. *The sixth element is follow-up.* People visit your site, email you, ask or answer some questions. Guerrillas respond to their email, stay in touch.

7. *The seventh element is promotion.* You must promote your site online by registering with search engines and linking with other sites, while

promoting it offline in mass media, mailings, wherever your name appears.

8. *The eighth element is maintenance.* Unlike other marketing, a website requires constant changing, updating, freshening, renewing. Like a baby.

It was once believed that websites had to be long to be valuable, but the increased awareness of the precious nature of time is causing online marketers to rethink this concept. Websites narrowly targeted to specific groups are brief and valuable. Guerrillas know the value of being concise.

An overall website may be vast, but within it are tiny segments targeted with precision for small niches. In this way, huge Guerrilla companies can have the warmth and close connection of small Guerrilla start-ups.

Once you've got even the spark of a notion to go online, let that spark ignite thoughts of how you'll promote your site. Have the insight to know this means thinking imaginatively about two worlds.

The first is the online world, where you'll think in terms of multiple links to other sites, in terms of banners leading to your site, search engines directing browsers to your site, postings on forums alerting surfers to your site, chat conferences heralding your site, recommendations of your site by internet powers, emailing to parties demonstrably interested in learning about the topics covered on your site, writing articles for other sites in return for links back to your site, mentioning your site in your email signature, advertising online to entice people to your site, preparing an online version of your press kit to publicize your site online, and connecting with as many other online entities as possible, all in a quest to make your site part of the online community, an internet landmark to your prospects, a not-be-missed feature of the web.

The second world in which your imagination should run rampant in a mission to achieve top-of-the-mind awareness of your site is the offline world. Most of the population of the real world still resides there. That's where they continue to get most of their information — for now. And that's where you've got to let them know of your online site — teeming with information that can shower them with benefits — for their business or their lives or both.

Tout your site in your ads, on stationery, on your business cards, on signs, on brochures, fliers, Yellow Pages ads, advertising specialties, package, business forms, gift certificates, reprints of PR articles, in your, newsletter, and classified ads. Mention it in your radio spots, on television. More than one company now has a jingle centered on their website. Never neglect to direct folks to your site in direct mail letters and postcards, in all your faxes, almost anywhere your name appears. If the world begins to think that your last name is dotcom, you're going about your offline promotional activities in the right way.

Some companies think that by including their site in tiny letters at the bottom of their ad or by flashing it at the end of their TV commercial, they're taking care of offline promotion. They're not. All they're doing is going through the motions. Talk about your website the same way you'd talk about your kid — with pride, enthusiasm and joy. Make people excited about your site because they can see your pride. Will local or industry newspapers write about your online site? Of course they will if you make it fascinating enough for their readers. That's your job. Promotion will get them to your site. Killer content will get them to make return trips.

What people want online is a question Guerrillas ask themselves a lot. Whether it's for fun or work or something else, understanding a consumer's motives once he or she logs on is a necessity. But the experts don't seem to agree on what people want. Some folks see the web as a vast, new field for advertising messages, assuming that while people may want to do something else, if we can entice them with flash, we can sort of trick them into paying attention to our products and services.

Guess what. That's not gonna happen.

Other folks seem to subscribe to the notion that people online are looking for entertainment on the Internet and therefore they construct messages aimed at persuading while playing. And, in other cases, the time-honored direct-response model wins out: Grab people when you can, get 'em to take an action, and then market, market, market. The answer may be that the consumer has and wants a lot more control than we give him/her credit for.

Today, webmasters are in control. Sort of. In a perfect cyber world, people will be in control. Sort of.

Two recent studies shed light upon this dilemma. One was conducted by Zatso. The other was conducted by the Pew Research Center, Zatso and Pew. Those guys didn't spend much time reading "how-to-name-your-company" books, I guess. Still, both of their studies illuminated the answer as to what people want to do online.

The answer, as most answers, is very utilitarian: People want to accomplish something online.

They're not aimless surfers hoping to discover a cyber treasure. Instead, the average Net user turns out to be a goal-oriented person interested in finding information and communicating with others ◻ in doing something he or she set out to do.

Look at the Zatso study. "A View of the 21st Century News Consumer" looked at people's news reading habits on the web. It revealed that reading and getting news was the most popular online activity after email. The Guerrilla thinks, "That means email is number one. How might I capitalize on that?"

One out of three respondents reported that they read news online every day, with their interests expanding geographically ◻ local news was of the most interest, U.S. news the least.

Personalization was seen as a benefit, too. Seventy-five percent of respondents said that they wanted news on demand and nearly two out of three wanted personalized news. The subjects surveyed liked the idea that they, not some media outlet, controlled the news they saw. They feel they're better equipped to select what they want to see than a professional editor. Again, control seems to be the issue. Again, Guerrillas think of ways to market by putting the prospect in control.

The Pew Research Center study revealed that regular net users were more connected with their friends and family than those who didn't use the Internet on a regular basis.

Almost two-thirds of the 3,500 respondents said they felt that email brought them closer to family and friends ◻ significant when combined with the fact that 91 percent of them used email on a regular basis. That's 91 percent. It took VCRs 25 years to achieve such market penetration.

What did people in this study seem to be doing online when they weren't doing email? Half were going online regularly to purchase products and services, and nearly 75 percent were going online to search for information about their hobbies or purchases they were planning to make. 64 percent of respondents visited travel sites, and 62 percent visited weather-related sites. Over half did educational research, and 54 percent were hunting for data about health and medicine.

A surprising 47 percent regularly visited government websites, and 38 percent researched job opportunities. Instant messaging was used by 45 percent of these users, and a third of them played games online.

Even with all the hype in the media, only 12 percent said they traded stocks online. What does this mean to e-marketers in tough times? It means that if you're constructing a site for goal-oriented consumers, you'd better make sure you can help facilitate their seeking. Rather than focus on entertainment, flash, and useless splash screens, the most effective sites are those that help people get the information they want when they need it. Straightforward data, information that invites comparison and straight talk are going to win the day.

A client buddy of mine showed me his website which heralds his retail location and attempts to sell nothing online. He said it has been the biggest moneymaker in the history of his 35-year-old company. Then he apologized for its lack of glitter and special effects. He asked how his site could be so successful even though it lacked anything to add razzmatazz and dipsydazzle. Now you know the answer.

GUERRILLA EXERCISE:

1. Write down the three questions you are asked most by your prospects and customers. The answers to those questions should be the starting point for the content on your website.

2. Answer this question: why do you want a website in the first place? The more focused your answer, the more valuable your website will be to you.

3. List what you have on your website that will involve visitors? Is it a free newsletter to which they might subscribe? A sweepstakes they may enter? A daily or weekly tip that is emailed to them regularly?

GUERRILLA ACTION STEPS:

A. Make a list of the other media you'll use to promote your online presence.

B. Review the eight steps necessary to create a winning website and ask yourself if you've paid enough attention to all eight. Put a checkmark next to each of the eight that you've emphasized.

Planning

Content

Design

Involvement

Production

Follow-up

Promotion

Maintenance

Don't forget, you must equally emphasize all eight ¤ or else.

Guerrilla Marketing
In Tough Times: Part XI

The Freebies That Can Lead To Serious Profits

These days, there seem to be two kinds of businesses: givers and takers. Giver businesses are quick to give freebies to customers and prospects. The freebies may be gifts, but more likely come in the form of information. The right information is worth more than a gift and often even worth far more than money.

In fact I've added a new personality trait to my list of characteristics possessed by successful guerrillas. I've always known they were blessed with infinite patience and fertile imaginations. I've written in awe of their acute sensitivity and their admirable ego strength. I've raved about their aggressiveness in marketing and their penchant for constant learning.

Now, I'm impressed, but not surprised, at their generosity. They are, every single one of them, generous souls who seem to gain joy by giving things away, by taking their customers and prospects beyond satisfaction and into true bliss. They learn what those people want and need and then they try to give them what they want and need absolutely free.

The result? Delighted prospects who become customers and delighted customers who become repeat and referral customers. Those are huge payoffs during the days of a bear market.

What kind of things do guerrilla marketers give away for free? Let's start with a list of 10 and your mind will be primed to dream up 10 more:

1. They give gift certificates to their own business, whether the certificates are for products or services.

2. They give printed brochures to anybody who requests one.

3. They give electronic brochures, on audio and video, once again to people who ask for them. And they are quick to offer their free brochures in their other marketing.

4. They give money to worthy causes and let their prospects and customers know that they support a noble cause, enabling these people to support the same endeavor.

5. They give free consultations and never make them seem like sales presentations. They truly try to help their prospects.

6. They give free seminars and clinics because they realize that if their information is worthwhile, it will attract the right kind of people to them.

7. They give free demonstrations to prove without words the efficacy of their offerings.

8. They give tours of their offices or of work they've accomplished elsewhere, again transcending any standard marketing tools they might employ.

9. They give free credit reports and appraisals because they know that such generosity is the equivalent of purchasing a new customer at a very low price.

10. They give invaluable information on their website, realizing that such data will bring their customers and prospects back for more, thereby intensifying their relationships.

In addition to these 10, guerrillas are highly creative in dreaming up what they might give for free. Of course, many advertising specialties such as calendars, scratchpads, mouse pads and ballpoint pens are emblazoned with their names and theme lines, but they seem to exercise extra creativity as well.

Case in point: When an apartment building went up, signs proudly proclaimed that you get "Free Auto Grooming" when you sign a lease. Soon the occupancy rate was 100 percent. The salary they paid the guy who washed the tenants' cars once a week was easily covered by the difference between 100 percent occupancy and 71 percent occupancy, the usual occupancy rate in that neighborhood.

That means your task is clear: Think of what might attract prospects and make customers happy. Be creative. Be generous. Then, be prepared for a reputation embracing generosity, customer service, and sincere caring.

Today's customers are attracted to giver companies and repelled by taker companies. What kind of company is yours?

During an economic downturn is the time to think freely. This is the time to think as hard as you can of what you can give away to your prospects for free. If you can possibly *give* away your product or service for a limited time, you have a good chance to habituate your prospects to your offering and a great chance to prove your service superiority. The idea behind this strategy is: give your prospects an ownership experience for free.

If you can enable your prospects to feel like your customers, you're acting just like a guerrilla marketer. You're in business because you offer a product or service that delivers desirable benefits. You're in business because you're better than many of your competitors. You're in business because you want to earn hefty profits consistently.

As a Guerrilla, you surpass customer satisfaction and allow those who patronize your business to experience customer bliss. They can tell how conscientious you are by means of your follow-up and the way you pay attention to details in their life and business. Customers of guerrillas are as contented as customers can get.

That's why you must give serious consideration to transforming all of your prospects into customers. If they won't do it by purchasing what you have to offer, regardless of your investment in marketing, perhaps they'll purchase what you have to offer if they first can try it at absolutely no cost.

If they have the experience of owning what you offer, they'll understand the advantages of being your customer. And then, they'll be far more likely to actually make the purchase.

This means that your prime marketing investment will be your freebie. It will be a limited time use of your product or a limited time use of your service. You'll be giving those valuable things away for free, risking that you'll get nothing in return. But if you're confident in your quality and service, that risk is minimized.

Of course, you can always give gift certificates, brochures, free consultations, free demos, free seminars, free tours and a wealth of free information on your website.

The highest form of that creativity is displayed when they give for free what they ordinarily sell. Hotmail attracted more than ten million customers for its free email service. Now, that service is supported by advertising. By ending each free email from the sender with an offer for free email for the recipient, Hotmail used word-of-mouse to the ultimate.

It's true that some bozos will sign up for your freebie and then you'll never hear from them again. But many customers will be so impressed by your quality and service, your caring and dedication, that they'll end up making the purchase you want them to make. Many will become lifelong customers, making you forget those free-loading bozos entirely.

The investment of your free product or service for a limited time must be measured against your current marketing investment. But if you're a Guerrilla, your quality and service will prove more than anything you can ever say in a marketing context. Your customers truly enjoy being your customers. Now, they know why you are so confident in your offering. Nothing can substitute for an actual ownership experience.

I realize that all companies cannot give what they sell for free, not even for a limited time. But if you can see daylight in giving your offering for free, you might lift your marketing to the highest level while forming bonds that might otherwise have never been established.

GUERRILLA EXERCISE:

1. List the things you currently give away at no cost.

2. List the other things you can, but currently do not give away.

3. List the businesses you patronize -- listing only those which gave you something for free.

GUERRILLA ACTION STEPS:

A. List the free information supplied on your website. For example, there is a list of Guerrilla Marketing articles on my own website at www.davidlhancock.com. Promoting those free articles attract visitors to my site.

B. List the kind of information your customers and prospects would most appreciate, then try to supply it at no cost on your website -- or even in printed form.

C. Put a check next to the items you currently offer for free:

Newsletter

Consultations

Demonstrations

Credit Reports and Appraisals

Trial Offers

Seminars and Clinics

Talks at Clubs and Associations

DAVID L. HANCOCK

Guerrilla Marketing
In Tough Times: Part XII

Getting Extra Mileage From Your Marketing And From Email

D on't limit your marketing merely to the media you're using. Market it all over the place. Anything worth promoting is worth cross-promoting. During the trying days of a rugged economy, this is a crucial strategy.

Guerrillas know that all the media work better if they're supported by the other media. Put your website onto your TV commercial. Mention your advertising in your direct mail. Refer to your direct mail in your telemarketing. Plant the seeds of your offering with some kinds of marketing and fertilize them with other kinds.

You're not really promoting unless you're cross-promoting. Your trade show booth will be far more valuable to you if you promote it in trade magazines and with fliers put under the doors of hotels near the trade show. Guerrillas try to market their marketing.

Your prospects, being humans, are eclectic people. They pay attention to a lot of media so you can't depend on a mere one medium to motivate a purchase. You've got to introduce a notion, remind them of it, say it again, then repeat it in different words somewhere else. That's how guerrilla survive. They combine several media. They say in their ads, "Call or write for our free brochure."

They say in their *Yellow Pages* ad, "Get even more details at our website." They enclose a copy of their magazine ad in their mailing. They blow up a copy to use as a sign. Their website features their print ads.

Guerrillas are quick to mention their use of one medium while using another because they realize that people equate broad scale marketing with quality and success. They know that people trust names they've heard of much more than strange and new names, and guerrillas are realistic enough to know that people miss most marketing messages ▫ often intentionally. The remote control is not only a way to save their steps but also a method of eliminating marketing messages.

No matter how glorious their newspaper campaign may be, guerrillas realize that not all of their prospects read the paper so they've got to get to these people in another way. No matter how dazzling their website, it's like a grain of sand in a desert if it's not pointed out to an unknowing and basically uncaring public.

Cross-promoting in the media is another way to accomplish the all-important task of repetition. One way to repeat yourself and implant your message is to say it over and over again. Another way is to say it in several different places. Guerrillas try to do both. Nothing is left to chance. If you saw a *Yellow Pages* ad that made you an offer from a company you've never heard of and another with the same offer except that the ad said, "As advertised on television," you'd probably opt for the second because of that added smidgen of credibility. I rest my case.

The psychology of marketing requires basic knowledge of human behavior. Human beings do not like making decisions in a hurry and are not quick to develop relationships. They certainly do want relationships, but they've been stung in the past and they don't want to be stung again.

They have learned well to distrust much marketing because of its proclivity to exaggeration. All too many times they've read of a sale at a store and learned that only a tiny selection of items were on sale. They've been bamboozled more times than you'd think by the notorious fine print on contracts. And they've been high-pressured by more than one salesperson.

That's why they process your marketing communications in their unconscious minds, eventually arriving at their decisions because of an emotional reason even though they may say they are deciding based on logic. They factor a lot about you into their final decision □ how long they've heard of you, where your marketing appears, how it looks and feels to them, the quality of your offer, your convenience or lack of it, what others have said about you, and most of all, how your offering can be of benefit to their lives.

Although they state that they now want what you're selling, and they do it in a very conscious manner, you can be sure they were guided by their unconscious minds. The consistent communicating of your benefits, your message and your name has penetrated their sacred unconscious mind. They've come to feel that they can trust you and so they decide to buy.

Any pothole in their road to purchasing at this point might dissuade them. They call to make an inquiry and they are treated shabbily on the phone? You've lost them. Do they access your website for more information and either find no website or find one littered with self-praise You've lost them. They visit you and feel pressured or misunderstood? They're gone.

You've got to realize that the weakest point in your marketing can derail all the strong points. Excellence through and through, start to finish, is what people have come to expect from businesses, and these days, they won't settle for less. The insight you must have is that marketing is a 360 degree process and you've got to do it right from all angles at all times. When it comes to marketing, people have built-in alarm systems, and any shady behavior on your part sets the bells to clanging, the sirens screaming.

It is very difficult to woo a person from the company they use right now to your company. Although they are loathe to change, they do change. And when they do, they patronize businesses that understand the psychology of human beings and the true nature of marketing.

During tough times, Guerrillas are very attuned to free methods of marketing. They are well aware that free marketing exists in its most free state as email, which is far more than merely letters with free postage.

Mark Twain said he never let his schooling interfere with his education. Regardless of your schooling, there's little chance it covered what technology makes possible today. If you took a course in how computers can aid your marketing, the first insight you would have gained would be into the profitability for you if you become savvy about email.

When you think of email, don't compare it with snail mail because it's considerably different. In fact, it is such an improvement on old-fashioned mail delivery that the U.S. Postal service now uses it, and today there is a lot more email being sent daily than snail mail. Soon, half of all bills and payments will be sent electronically. In 2000 two-thirds of Social Security checks, tax refunds and other federal payments were sent electronically.

In fact, the U.S. Postal Service is now in serious trouble because of the vast amount of information transmitted via the Internet. For much of this, Guerrillas owe a tip of their propeller beanie to Ray Tomlinson who invented email in l971.

You can use email in your marketing in ways that will make your customers delighted to be doing business with you. Guerrillas love email but hate junk email, known as spamming. Their affinity to email is because they can deliver their messages instantly and to anywhere in the world if the recipients are online, as more and more of them are with each word I type. That means email saves you time in communicating and money that you used to spend on postage. It can also help save trees on the planet because it is so delightfully paperless.

Each recipient can read your email on screen or print and save it just as with a standard letter, which does use paper. But you don't have to print and save your email, saving you the cost of paper and the convenience of space. Save it in your computer. Make copies as you need them. All your files and memos can be kept in one convenient location. Each one is dated and timed. Many experts feel that for all the great things about being online, email is the most valuable of all computer applications.

Email also helps you save on the cost of courier service and faxing. Use it to send brief messages or long documents, to send black and white communications or colorful, beautifully designed materials. It's easy for you and easy for the person who receives your email.

Who should that be? People who want to receive it, that's who. Find their names on your customer list, in the newsgroups to which you belong, in chat rooms where they're talking about your industry, possibly even your company. Although email isn't free, because you need a computer and an Internet connection, it's far less expensive than telephoning, mailing or faxing. When using it, keep your message as brief as possible because people read computer screens differently than letters. They know being online saves time, so they don't want to waste time reading long things. As Thomas Jefferson said, "Never use two words when one word will do."

You're aware, as all Guerrillas are, of how technology can strengthen your marketing. You must also be aware of its limitations and of the new advancements that are taking place at breakneck speed. Don't let those advancements overwhelm you. Very little becomes obsolete, but nearly everything becomes improved.

Technology, for all the wondrous things about it, can also be a major distraction and a drain on your time if you focus on the technology itself rather than on the benefits it can bring to your business.

As *Net Benefits* author Kim Elton reminds us, "Business is life and life is messy. Like a kitchen sink full of dirty dishes, you know that when you've finally cleaned them up, someone will burn a tuna casserole and you'll be back in sudsy water up to your elbows with a Brillo pad in no time. But if the kids are growing up healthy and strong □ and helping out with the dishes now and then □ it's all worth the effort. Soon you'll get a dishwasher and you can shift the mess from the sink to the dishwasher. The dishes still have to be cleaned. The technology eases the labor and takes away some of the pain, but it doesn't relieve the duty."

That's the insight that I want you to take from this section and from this book. Technology helps with the job but doesn't do the job. That's your task. In order for you to understand how technology can help you, it's not necessary for you to learn the technical jargon, the nerdy part of technology. But you must comprehend the impact of technology and the ways it can transform a squirt gun into a cannon.

To cash in on the transformation, you must be in close touch with your needs. Technology will help you meet them. You must know how best to utilize the technology in which you've invested to get the maximum benefit for the money you've put forth. You've got to recognize hype for just what it is and solid science for just what it is.

You wouldn't dream of running a business without using a telephone. The computer will be just as endemic as phones. Using technology will be as easy as making a phone call. Investment research company Robertson Stephens stated it this way:

"Communicating is becoming the primary role of computers after four decades of number crunching. We stand at a technology crossroads and are witnessing a technological metamorphosis... computers, originally designed for number crunching and applied to computing tasks for nearly 50 years, will be used in the future primarily for communicating." The future is now the present.

Now, you know how to market during tough times.

GUERRILLA EXERCISE:

1. List the ways you currently market your marketing.

2. Dig deep into your mind a list three other ways you can market your marketing.

3. Prepare a plan for using email during the next year. Putting it into writing helps it transform into a reality.

GUERRILLA ACTION STEPS:

A. Begin compiling a list of people to whom you'll send email. Get that list from your customer list, from people who will trade lists with you, from people who have registered for something from your website, and from your fusion marketing partners. Nobody appreciates spam, but almost everyone appreciates email targeted at their interests.

B. Make a list, based upon this course, of the marketing tactics you will begin to employ to make waves during tough times. Times may be tough for others -- but tough times are golden opportunities for guerrillas.

DAVID L. HANCOCK

What is A Guerrilla Mortgage Broker?

The Guerrilla mortgage broker knows that the journey *is* the goal.

They also realize that they are in control of their enterprise, not the other way around, and that if they are dissatisfied with their journey, they are missing the point of the journey itself.

Unlike old-fashioned enterprises, which often required huge sacrifices for the sake of the goal, Guerrilla enterprises place the goal of a pleasant journey ahead of the mere notion of sacrifices.

The Guerrilla mortgage broker achieves balance from the very start.

They build free time into their work schedule so that balance is part of their enterprise.

They respect their leisure time as much as their work time, never allowing too much of one to interfere with the other. Traditional mortgage brokers always placed work ahead of leisure and showed no respect for their own personal freedom. Guerrillas cherish their freedom as much as their work.

The Guerrilla mortgage broker is not in a hurry.

A false need for speed frequently undermines even the best conceived strategies. Haste makes waste and sacrifices quality. The Guerrilla is fully aware that patience is their ally, and they have planned intelligently to eliminate most emergencies that call for moving fast. Their pace is always steady but never rushed.

The Guerrilla mortgage broker uses stress as a benchmark.

If they feel any stress, they know they must be going about things in the wrong way. Guerrilla mortgage brokers do not accept stress as part of doing business and recognize any stress as a warning sign that something's the matter – in the work plan of the Guerrilla or in the business itself.

Adjustments are made to eliminate the cause of the stress rather than the stress itself.

The Guerrilla mortgage broker looks forward to work.

They have a love affair with their work and consider themselves blessed to be paid for doing the work they do. They are good at their work, energizing their passion in a quest to learn more and improve their understanding of it, thereby increasing their skills. The Guerrilla mortgage broker doesn't think about retirement, for never would they want to stop doing work they love.

The Guerrilla mortgage broker has no weaknesses.

They are effective in every aspect of their enterprise because they have filled in the gaps between their strengths and talents with people who abound in the prowess they lack. They are very much the team player and team up with Guerrillas like themselves who share the team spirit and possess complementary skills.

They value their teammates as much as old-fashioned mortgage brokers valued their independence.

The Guerrilla mortgage broker is fusion-oriented.

They are always on the alert to fuse their business with other enterprises in town, in America, in the world. They are willing to combine marketing efforts, production skills, information, leads, mailing lists and anything else to increase their effectiveness and marketing reach while reducing the cost of achieving those goals.

Their fusion efforts are intentionally short-term and rarely permanent. In their business relationships, instead of thinking marriage, they think fling.

The Guerrilla mortgage broker does not kid him or herself.

They know that if they overestimate their own abilities, they run the risk of skimping on the quality they represent to their customers, employees, investors, suppliers and fusion partners.

They force themselves to face reality on a daily basis and realize that all of their business practices must always be evaluated in the glaring light of what is really happening, instead of what should be happening.

The Guerrilla mortgage broker lives in the present.

They are well-aware of the past and very enticed by the future, but the here and now is where they reside, embracing the technologies of the present, leaving future technologies on the horizon. Future technologies belong on the horizon until later, when they are ripe and ready. They are alert to the new, wary of the avant-garde, and only wooed from the old by improvement – not merely change.

The Guerrilla mortgage broker understands the precious nature of time.

They don't buy into the old lie that time is money and know in their heart that time is far more important than money. They know that instead, time is life. They are aware that their customers and prospects feel the same way about time, so they respect it and wouldn't dare waste it.

As a practicing Guerrilla, they are the epitome of efficiency, but never let it interfere with their effectiveness.

The Guerrilla mortgage broker always operates according to a plan.

They know who they are, where they are going, and how they will get there. They are prepared, know that anything can and will happen, and can deal with the barriers to their success because their plan has foreseen and shown exactly how to surmount them. The Guerrilla reevaluates their plan regularly and does not hesitate to make changes in it, though commitment to the plan is part of their very being.

The Guerrilla mortgage broker is flexible.

They are guided by a strategy for success, and know the difference between a guide and a master. When it is necessary for change, the Guerrilla changes, accepting change as part of the status quo, not ignoring or battling it. They are able to adapt to new situations, realize service is whatever their customers want it to be, and know inflexible things become brittle and break.

The Guerrilla aims for results more than growth.

They are focused upon profitability and balance, vitality and improvement, value and quality more than size and growth. Their plan calls for steadily increasing profits without a sacrifice of personal time, so their actions are oriented to hitting those targets instead of growing for the sake of growth alone. They are wary of becoming large and do not equate hugeness with excellence.

The Guerrilla mortgage broker is dependent upon many people.

They know that the age of the lone wolf mortgage broker, independent and proud of it, has passed. The Guerrilla is very dependent upon their fusion business partners, their employees, their customers, their suppliers, and their mentors. They got where they are with their own wings, their own determination, their own smarts, and, as a Guerrilla, with a little help from a lot of friends.

The Guerrilla mortgage broker is constantly learning.

A seagull flies in circles in the sky, looking for food in an endless quest. When it finally finds the food, the seagull lands, then eats its fill. When it has completed the meal, the seagull returns to the sky, only to fly in circles again, searching for food although it has eaten. Humans have only one instinct that compares: the need for constant learning. Guerrilla mortgage brokers have this need in spades.

The Guerrilla mortgage broker is passionate about work.

They have an enthusiasm for what they do that is apparent to everyone who sees their work. This enthusiasm spreads to everyone who works with them, even to their customers. In its purest form, this enthusiasm is best expressed as the word passion ▫ an intense feeling that burns within and manifested in the devotion they demonstrate towards their business.

The Guerrilla mortgage broker is focused on the goal.

They know balance does not come easily, and they must rid themselves of the values and expectations of their ancestors. To do this, they must remain focused upon their journey, seeing the future clearly while concentrating upon the present. They are aware that the minutiae of life and business can distract them. As a result they do what is necessary to make those distractions only momentary.

The Guerrilla mortgage broker is disciplined about the tasks at hand.

They are keenly aware that every time they write a task on their daily calendar, it is a promise they are making to themselves.

As a Guerrilla who does not kid him or herself, they keep those promises, knowing that the achievement of their goals will be more than an adequate reward for their discipline. They find it easy to be disciplined because of the payback offered by the leisure that follows.

The Guerrilla mortgage broker is well-organized at home and at work.

They know they waste valuable time looking for items that have been misplaced, so they organize as they work and as new work comes to them. Their sense of organization is fueled by the efficiency that results from it. While they are always organized, the Guerrilla never squanders precious time by over organizing.

The Guerrilla mortgage broker has an upbeat attitude.

Because they know life is unfair, problems arise, to err is human, and the cool shall inherit the Earth, they manage to take obstacles in stride, keeping their perspective and their sense of humor. Their ever-present optimism is grounded in an ability to perceive the positive side of things, recognizing the negative, but never dwelling there.

Their positivity is contagious.

Until now, no marketing association in existence could make a business bulletproof. But once again, Jay Conrad Levinson, the most respected marketer in the world, has broken new ground. The Guerrilla Marketing Association is quite literally a blueprint for business immortality.

You've got to have it!

Join right now before your competition does at www.davidlhancock.com/gma.

About the Author

David L. Hancock has been in marketing his entire life. He is an accomplished Mortgage Banker, Public Speaker, Author, Certified Guerrilla Marketing Coach and Publisher.

As a Mortgage Banker and Guerrilla Marketing Coach, Hancock knows what its like to compete in the marketplace for a prospects time.

Other titles by David L. Hancock:

✓ *The Secrets of Master Marketing: Discover how to Produce an Endless Stream of New, Repeat and Referral Business by Using These Powerful Marketing and Customer Service Secrets*

Morgan James Publishing ISBN: 0-9746133-0-4

✓ *Believe & Succeed: The Strangest Law of the Universe!*

Morgan James Publishing ISBN: 0-9760901-0-4

✓ *The State of The Union: A tribute to Ronald Reagan*

Morgan James Publishing ISBN: 0-9758570-3-7

✓ *Affiliate Cash Flow Marketing: A Dirt Cheap Marketing System That Makes Ordinary Affiliates Top Producers In 12-18 Months!*

Imprint Books ISBN: 1-5910967-3-1

✓ *How to Join the eBay Game and WIN!: An e-biz in every closet. Get into Auction Action! Start and Grow a profitable Internet Auction Business.*

Imprint Books: 1-5910967-4-X

Available in fine bookstores everywhere and on line at Amazon.com

DAVID L. HANCOCK

Printed in the United Kingdom
by Lightning Source UK Ltd.
110019UKS00001B/203